JB JOSSEY-BASS™
A Wiley Brand

Basics of Nonprofit Publicity

Winning Strategies for News Releases, Press Conferences and Media Relations

Scott C. Stevenson, Editor

WILEY

Basics of Nonprofit Publicity:

Winning Strategies for News Releases, Press Conferences and Media Relations

Published by

Stevenson, Inc.

P.O. Box 4528 • Sioux City, Iowa • 51104

Phone 712.239.3010 • Fax 712.239.2166

www.stevensoninc.com

Basics of Nonprofit Publicity

Basics of Nonprofit Publicity

CRAFTING COMPELLING NEWS RELEASES AND FEATURES

There's a reason it's often said that any publicity is good publicity — getting out the word about your organization is the first step in winning donors, recruiting volunteers, attracting members and achieving a range of other mission-critical goals. The following tips and advice will help you tell your agency's story in ways that will interest readers and attract media outlets.

Grab Attention With Every Story

To make sure you offer stories people want to read, include these key elements, says Teresa Scalzo, director of publications, Carleton College (Northfield, MN) and award-winning editor of the quarterly magazine, Carleton College Voice:

1. First and foremost, you must have good stories.

2. Second, you need good writers. Treat a good writer like gold, whether he/she is a staff writer or a freelancer.

3. Photography and/or illustration. "Good photography is one of the surest ways to turn skimmers into readers," she says. "A compelling photograph will stop a skimmer in his tracks and get him to pay closer attention to the story."

4. Design. Hire a great designer who understands magazine design.

5. Paper and printing. "Producing magazines is hugely expensive. Don't squander your investment by shirking your responsibility at the very end of the process," says Scalzo. "Choose a printer with a solid reputation (and, ideally, one who has experience printing magazines) and work with your sales rep to choose the best quality paper you can afford."

Source: Teresa Scalzo, Director of Publications and Editor, Carleton College Voice, Carleton College, Northfield, MN. Phone (507) 222-5423. E-mail: tscalzo@carleton.edu

Copywriting Tips: Get to the Point Quickly

When you create a brochure, flyer, Web page or e-mail with the purpose of getting recipients to actively take part in your mission, here are some tips for making a compelling point quickly.

Describe immediate needs. Highlight your most pressing priority (e.g., donations, volunteer help) and how lack of those things is impacting your ability to serve more people. Point out ways your organization fills a unique niche in the community that no one else does.

Use independent statistics that support your case. When you can cite outside sources who agree you are uniquely qualified to meet certain community needs, readers you hope to persuade can more easily see that their time and/or money is being directed to a specific cause and goal.

List ways people can support you. Show readers that they have choices ranging from donating and volunteering to joining your Facebook fan page and helping promote your cause. Concentrate on your most urgent need first, but include as many possibilities as practical to ensure that more potential supporters find an agreeable fit.

Keep copy brief. Offer enough details to pique interest in your organization and generate calls for more information. When you can speak to intereste parties directly and answer their specific questions, chances of gaining some level of commitment increase dramatically.

Include a human element. Lisa the honor student who can't attend college without scholarship assistance, or Mike the injured war veteran who needs home healthcare to live independently help put a face to your cause. Lisa and Mike can speak directly to your readers by explaining how they rely on you for their continued progress.

Spin Familiar Stories New Ways

To the media, the construction of a building might not generate that much interest. To overcome this hurdle and get the publicity you seek, take a new angle on the way you pitch the story.

Here are some fresh ideas for doing so from Joan Stewart, media relations consultant (Port Washington, WI):

✓ **Go Green:** Explain how you are using green materials in your project and how it benefits the environment.

✓ **Cut Costs:** Did you take a unique approach to financing your project, especially when people are doing without everywhere in the United States?

✓ **Go Viral:** Take photos and turn them into a Flickr slideshow to share your progress with the media, volunteers and donors. Better yet, shoot a short video explaining aspects of the project and put it on your Facebook page or share it on YouTube.

Source: Joan Stewart, Media Relations Consultant & Author, The Publicity Hound, Port Washington, WI. Phone (262) 284-7451. E-mail: jstewart@publicityhound.com. Website: http://www.PublicityHound.com. Blog: http://www.PublicityHound.net

Let Volunteers, Supporters Tell Your Organization's Story

Sharing your organization's story with the public is more than a matter of selecting events and writing press releases. Remember that every person who dedicates his or her time to your mission sees your story differently. Use that knowledge as you consider unique ways to tell your story:

✓ **Look for unique messengers**. The most compelling people are not always public speakers. Seek out those who have meaningful relationships with your organization and make a video or write a short story about them.

✓ **Let your supporters tell your story**. Host a 100-words-or-less contest where they can tell why they appreciate your programs and services that you can use in advertisements, in publications or on your website.

✓ **Clearly define your call to action**. While you may have a variety of ways to tell your organization's story, focus on and identify one or more intriguing common threads (such as job training for domestic violence survivors) and turn it into a feature article to submit to local publications to use at any time.

✓ **Ask volunteers to submit videos**. Many people feel comfortable and candid when they can create their own video in their own environment describing why they became involved with your cause. Provide a time limit and two or three questions for them to answer. Post them on your blogs, social media outlets and website.

✓ **Focus on honesty and realism**. Overselling your mission can defeat your purpose if success stories don't ring true. People recognize that small victories for one of your beneficiaries can lead to life-changing long-term accomplishments. Be proud of being a small but significant step in someone's journey and share it proudly.

✓ **Find new audiences for your story**. All of your volunteers, clients and supporters know people who are not familiar with your programs. Seek out some of those supporters to speak to members of their churches, civic clubs or academic groups and invite those who show interest to visit your facility for a tour.

Consider These Techniques for Writing Vibrant Copy

Every organization has clients, patients, volunteers or students who have success stories related to the organization's mission. Deciding how to best tell those stories is the first step in sharing them with the public.

Consider these angles to determine the most effective means by which to share stories about persons benefiting from your mission:

❏ **Write an As-told-to article**. The subject can share his or her thoughts and experiences candidly in his/her own words, but leave the actual writing in the hands of a professional who can identify the most relevant aspects to include in the story.

❏ **Mix journal excerpts with editorial**. Some people enjoy keeping journals while they are going through medical challenges, rehabilitation, or as a way of handling life-changing events like the loss of a family member or a career change. When your organization has helped them through those times, an article that includes their thoughts at the time adds more dimension.

❏ **Interview involved staff**. While keeping your client or patient as the focus of your article, include comments from those who assisted him/her on the road to success. Members of the medical team who formulated the treatment plan, counselors who helped identify his/her true vocation or mentors who offered guidance can contribute to the overall story.

❏ **Take a photojournalism approach**. Pictures can tell a client's story in a highly personal way, showing struggle, determination, contemplation, teamwork, self-discovery and the joy of accomplishment. Once you have identified a potential success story, be there for important steps in his or her journey through your programs.

❏ **Create a video diary and article**. Reality television shows often give subjects video cameras, so they can record their concerns when film crews are off duty. Footage of your subjects sharing their thoughts the day before an important job interview or medical procedure, or their reactions the day after, can be combined with editorial for a fascinating online article.

Five Ways to Develop Features on Volunteers

One effective way to attract, retain and celebrate volunteers is to publicize the ways they serve your organization. Here are five fresh ideas for feature articles that will boost publicity about your organization while recognizing your volunteers:

1. **Interview the volunteer about his/her three most memorable experiences working for you.** When given the opportunity to recall why volunteers are dedicated to your organization, those hesitant about discussing themselves may enjoy telling about their triumphs, trials and emotions while on the job. They may have conquered a blizzard or taken a 20-hour shift during a crisis, and certainly touched the lives of those in your charity.

2. **Do a photo feature with brief captions and a short story.** Take a camera to capture volunteers doing work within your organization, but also follow them home for a picture in the garden or with family. Let photos tell the reader about your special volunteer's other life.

3. **Try a bullet-point at-a-glance format.** Use one good feature photo with unique questions for them to answer briefly. Volunteers could answer questions such as: "Which fictional character do you relate to most strongly?" or "What is your greatest indulgence?"

4. **Make the story a pleasant surprise.** Like the classic television show, "This Is Your Life," surprise an honoree with friends, family, teachers, role models and co-workers who share favorite stories and photos of the guest.

5. **Tell readers what they don't know about the volunteer.** Let the opening of your article describe some of the highlights and accomplishments the subject has achieved within your organization, but follow with "Ten Little-known Facts About…."

Avoid These Common Press Release Mistakes

Newsrooms get hundreds of press releases a day. It takes a well-crafted press release to get your nonprofit news coverage. Here are the four biggest press release issues, and guidance to help you master them:

✓ **Positioning the lead:** Newsroom decision makers may only have time to can your release. If you don't have an attention-grabbing headline and lead paragraph, you will get overlooked. After that, tell the reporter where to be and when.

✓ **Contact information:** Press contacts and phone numbers should be at the top of your release. Include your office line, cell phone and a second person to contact if you are not available.

✓ **Timing of news releases:** News is a 24/7 business, but most newsrooms are generally staffed from 9:30 a.m. to 10:30 p.m. And your key decision-makers work regular business hours. For that reason, send releases no later than 3 p.m. for next-day events.

✓ **Timing of events:** Most newsroom staffs are lean and most reporters may not report until 9:30 a.m. If you routinely hold events at 8:30 a.m., you may not get coverage. The same goes for an event that is too late in the day. Know the deadlines for newspaper, television and radio stations in your area and set your events accordingly.

Make the Most of Letters to the Editor

A letter to the editor of your local, regional or even a national newspaper or magazine is a simple way to raise awareness about your organization.

But this tried-and-tested communications method can be so much more than an awareness raiser. These ideas can help you make the most of your next letter to the editor:

1. **Have a point.** Using a letter to the editor to thank the community for their support of a fundraiser or event is OK, though it's important to make it relevant. Tie the need for your organization to current events. Include recently updated statistics that relate to your work or a timely issue that your organization is helping to address.

2. **Be an expert.** Use your knowledge and role to educate others about the headlines. Writing a letter offering more detailed information or advice about breaking news stories still gets your organization out there, while serving the community as a whole. It may even lead to additional exposure, if local reporters start to view you as an expert on specific subjects.

3. **Offer assistance.** If your organization provides assistance that can help people with a problem existing in your community, make sure to let them know that. Be the solution people can find in an unlikely place.

Whether written by yourself, your CEO/executive director, your board president or even a satisfied employee or client, keep the letter to the editor brief and memorable. Written well, a letter to the editor can be a powerful tool to help further your goals.

Websites Help News Releases Reach New Audiences

If you frequently create press releases on behalf of your member organization, consider posting them to a press release hosting site. Here is a sampling of websites that will give your releases broader attention:

- **Express Press Release Network** — www.Express-Press-Release.net. Fee for posting is $29 per press release.

- **PR.com** — www.pr.com. The Silver membership is free with enrollment and allows press release distribution and job posting opportunities. Offering enhanced benefits are the Gold membership ($199/year) and Platinum membership ($499/year).

- **1888 Press Release** — www.1888pressrelease.com. Enjoy free press release submission with enrollment, and five enhanced benefit plans ranging from $15 to $249 a year.

- **Free Press Release Center** — www.free-press-release-center.info. Registration is free and this site also offers press release writing services for an additional fee of $49.

- **Send2Press Newswire** — www.send2press.com. This site offers a variety of news writing and distribution services and offers nonprofits a significant discount when enrolling in a plan.

Website Tool Helps Get News Out

The website for the Monroe Carell Jr. Children's Hospital at Vanderbilt (Nashville, TN) features a news section with an extensive news release and general news search feature.

Web Manager Susan Kohari says the custom-built tool lets news and communications staff enter all information into one location using a tagging system and specific categories. They then use that information to determine where news items will show up on either of their two websites and populate their news homepage with stories of their choice.

The tool automatically sizes the photos and carries the teaser and story over from its original location.

Kohari says that creating the tool internally gave them specific advantages. "The news and communications department wanted their page to look more like a news site than the other Children's Hospital pages, and we were able to do that."

Check out the online search tool at: www.childrenshospital.vanderbilt.org/news

Source: Susan Kohari, Web Manager, Monroe Carell Jr. Children's Hospital at Vanderbilt, Nashville, TN. Phone (615) 322-3132. E-mail: susan.kohari@vanderbilt.edu

Make Testimonials Relevant, Specific to Audience Interests

Testimonials. They fill website margins and mailer pages. But do they really work?

They can — provided they are relevant to readers' interests and emphasize your organization's mission and values, says Nancy Schwartz, president of Nancy Schwartz & Company (Maplewood, NJ) and publisher of GettingAttention.org.

"The more information a testimonial contains about the person giving it, the more credible it will be," says Schwartz. "Name, title, organization and location are a must, and headshots are great when possible. Anything that helps prospective members feel connected to a peer, rather than an organization, is good."

To avoid bland or generic testimonials, include as many details as possible, she recommends. "Don't just say the chamber of commerce doubled your business in a year, show how it did it through specific services or programs. Show, don't tell, and always include specifics."

How should organizations go about getting testimonials?

"You don't want to ask for testimonials — those always sound either forced or insincere," says Schwartz. "Take elements of member feedback, say comments from an annual survey, and craft them into something really powerful. You start with raw comments, but you don't need to be shy about shaping those comments, so long as you get permission to do so."

Use testimonials wisely, she advises. Don't silo them into one page of your newsletter, brochure or website. Rather, integrate them throughout the text to underscore particular pieces of content. Consider placing them directly under subheadings as well as in sidebars to main stories of related content.

Schwartz' best tip on how to spice up testimonials? Use a headline phrase.

"Using a headline phrase to frame a testimonial can add tremendous value," she says. "For example, a testimonial for a volunteer program at a camp for kids with special needs might read, 'The toughest vacation you'll ever love.' It draws interest and makes the testimonial more immediately meaningful."

Source: Nancy Schwartz, Publisher, GettingAttention.org and President, Nancy Schwartz & Company, Maplewood, NJ. Phone (973) 762-0079. E-mail: Nancy@nancyschwartz.com. Websites: www.nancyschwartz.com; http://gettingattention.org

Basics of Nonprofit Publicity

ATTRACTING MEDIA INTEREST AND ATTENTION

Contacting the public directly has become easier and easier, but traditional media organizations such as television channels and radio stations remain the most efficient way of connecting with large numbers of individuals. Media-friendly pitches, productive relationships with media representatives, effective media relations committees and staff expert programs are just a few ways your organization can attract media interest and attention.

Grab the Media's Attention

Looking to gain media attention for your event? You may want coverage in your local newspaper, but wonder where to begin.

Rebecca Leaman, a blogger with Wild Apricot (Toronto, Ontario, Canada), asked a longtime editor of a community newspaper and a freelance reporter how to make news headlines.

Here, Leaman shares their insight into gaining media coverage for your event:

❏ **Get familiar with the publication.** Determine what kinds of stories the publication normally runs and if it typically uses press releases and photos with brief captions or human-interest features about local personalities.

❏ **Build a relationship with a reporter or editor.** Check back issues for local stories like yours and note the names of reporters involved. Establishing a relationship with one or two reporters may win you a champion when it comes to pitching stories.

❏ **Get to the point of your pitch.** Don't call with a rambling intro to your organization, working toward asking for a story. Instead, ask how to submit an item to the local events calendar or other specific column.

❏ **Tell a good story.** Never mind the do-it-yourself public relations advice about reverse pyramid structure and press release formats; hook them with a story that practically writes itself. If you have a brief elevator pitch to immediately plant a picture in a reporter's mind, you have a great shot at getting into print.

❏ **Check the editorial calendar.** Does the paper have regular features or seasonal issues that fit with your schedule of activities, events and fundraising campaigns? If so, pitch them!

❏ **Put together a media kit.** What can you do to make it easier for the reporter, editor and layout department? Provide press releases, artwork, photographs, logos, and other graphic elements, quotes from key individuals, contacts for more information and other assets that tell your story.

Source: Rebecca Leaman, Wild Apricot Blogger and Jay Moonah, Wild Apricot/Bonasource Inc., Toronto, Ontario, Canada. Phone (416) 410-4059. E-mail: jay@wildapricot.com. Website: www.wildapricot.com Blog: http://www.wildapricot.com/blogs/newsblog/default.aspx

Stand Out From Other Nonprofits to Your Media Partners

A long-term partnership with one of the local network affiliates in your area is a real win for your organization. The publicity potential is truly endless.

But what if your nonprofit is not the only group vying for the TV station's airtime? How do you stand out?

Here are two steps to take to give your nonprofit a competitive edge:

1. **Focus your initial pitch on how the partnership will benefit the television station.** This may sound backwards. After all, you want to further your nonprofit's mission. But you can't ignore that television is a highly competitive industry. Give the key decision makers examples of how the partnership will help get more

viewers tuned in to their product. For instance, if you have a large volunteer and donor base, suggest sending out an e-mail blast every time your organization is featured. In addition, provide the station with high profile opportunities to get their anchor talent involved in your events.

2. **Make it easy for the TV station.** Approach the TV officials with a clear plan of what you need and when. Do you want them to produce a spot to promote a charity event? If that is the case, come to the meeting with an idea for a script. If news coverage is what you want, bring a list of topics and potential interviews and even dates interviewees would be available.

Story-generating Ideas to Try

No news is good news — unless you want to keep your organization in the public eye. So how do you accomplish this when you are between major events? Try these methods to make news during slow times.

❏ **Revise your mission statement.** Your mission hasn't changed, but the language needs updating. Focus on new ways you use time-honored principles to meet current community needs. Your press release can reiterate an eagerness to remain flexible in changing times while maintaining continuity.

❏ **Consolidate programs into a fresh package.** If you offer several programs, combine those that complement each other into a new initiative to reintroduce to the public. For example, weekly bingo games, monthly pottery classes and transportation services might be called Sociable Seniors.

❏ **Get away from your desk and look for inspiration.** Are volunteers in the courtyard planting geraniums? Is construction in the parking lot inconveniencing patients or clients? Volunteers and flowers make a good photo or brief news video. Informing the media that you are temporarily moving your outpatient entrance to better serve visitors until construction is complete might get a news nibble, too.

❏ **Make business as usual look more interesting.** The head chef in your cafeteria proudly reports that he can't make enough of his gluten-free brownies to meet overwhelming staff and visitor demand. Invite a couple of reporters to sample them, or send the recipe or a sample box to local newspapers with food sections. There are similar hidden news gems in nearly every department if you make the effort to find them.

Raise Awareness With On-staff Experts

Your organization has a wealth of experts — teachers, health professionals or advisers — who may have a great deal to share with your community. Helping them spread their knowledge also helps bring positive attention to your nonprofit.

✓ **Start a speaker's bureau.** Create a series of general interest topics that fit your experts' skills, and develop brief biographies of each one.

✓ **Make them available to the media.** Send lists of experts and their fields to television stations, radio programs, newspaper section editors and business and trade publications. You can be the go-to person when they need sources.

✓ **Host or sponsor community workshops.** Summer fitness, babysitting safety, quick family meals, planning your annual budget are just a few examples of topics for spotlighting your experts while also providing a valuable service.

✓ **Start a mentoring program.** Your staff experts can help keep your organization in touch with younger constituents by serving as career mentors in their fields. Once you have several lined up, contact local schools to inform them of availability.

✓ **Suggest them as news feature subjects.** A pediatrics nurse takes time off to volunteer in Haiti. An avian specialist from the local zoo heads to the Gulf Coast to help rescue birds who have been harmed by oil in the wetlands. Keep up to date on what your co-workers are doing in their spare time. These are stories to be shared.

Boost Media Exposure With an Expert Program

At one level, the faculty expert program at Villanova University (Villanova, PA) is a simple thing: a website putting media representatives in touch with faculty members available for interview. But the program accomplishes far more than that, says Jonathan Gust, director of media relations.

The program "assists the media, but it also serves as a mechanism to increase institutional visibility and highlight the world-class strength of our faculty and staff," he says. "It's a way to regularly put our name in front of the public."

The media relations department, which launched the program shortly after its inception in 2007, schedules media interviews and provides background and guidance on which faculty experts could best speak on particular topics. It also works with key department heads to recruit faculty to the program. Over 150 professors currently participate, but Gust expects that number to double as the program continues to develop. At present, the program accommodates 20 to 25 request a week.

Each participating expert is listed by name, title, area of expertise and biographical overview on the program's website. Information on education, professional experience, publications and research is also provided.

All aspects of the site are tailored to the needs of media contacts, Gust says. "The goal is to create a one-stop media shop — the kind of place professionals like and would want to return to."

Because the faculty profiles need to be updated regularly, the program demands significant resources. But Gust says the effort is well worth the trouble. "The media is constantly looking for spokespeople to speak on areas of breaking news, and the faculty expert program positions us as a reliable and valuable resource."

Source: Jonathan Gust, Director of Media Relations, Villanova University, Villanova. PA. Phone (610) 519-6508. E-mail: jonathan.gust@villanova.edu. Website: www.villanova.edu/communication/media

Securing Media Coverage In Changing Media Market

With certain media markets dwindling, including doors closing on some newspapers, how do you make sure your story gets out?

"It's more important than ever to find a real point of differentiation in the news you're offering," says Nicole Pitaniello, assistant vice president for public relations, Albany Medical Center (Albany, NY).

Pitaniello says she used this strategy when pitching a story similar to one a local paper had already picked up on in brief. The pitch was about new technology that would enable people with certain neurological conditions to communicate better. The reporter was hesitant to follow through with a feature piece because of the prior story. Pitaniello says she convinced the reporter it would be worthwhile because of the value to the paper's readers.

"I argued that if one of my family members had one of these conditions and there was something out there that could help improve their quality of life, I'd want to know about it. And a story like the one I was pitching could make it real for people," Pitaniello says. "It's really all about selling them on why it's important for their readers to know this information, not why it's important ... to get your story told."

Source: Nicole Pitaniello, Assistant Vice President for Public Relations, Albany Medical Center, Albany, NY. Phone (518) 262-3421. E-mail: PitaniN@mail.amc.edu

Go Beyond the Media When Sending News Release Invites

Be sure any press conference surrounding a major gift or a campaign announcement includes a good number of people present.

The media's coverage of stories is influenced by the public's interest in them. A press conference with eight people present will receive different media coverage than one with 50 people there.

When sending an invitation to the news media, consider other audiences you want in the background — board members, employees, volunteers and such — and get on the phone to personally invite them to share in the good news as well.

Get Valuable TV Exposure for Your Cause

Every nonprofit organization has newsworthy events, but few promote them through TV exposure. This can be an exciting prospect. Don't be intimidated by TV. Your story idea does not have to be as earth shattering as the latest quake.

It helps if you have a unique angle, an interesting character or an out-of-the-ordinary theme. Most TV stations set aside daily free public service broadcast time. Some have special segments dedicated to interviewing an event organizer.

Here's how to get on the air:

✓ **Contact television stations.** From the community affairs director, request guidelines for submitting a story idea or publishing an event. Is it communicated by letter, e-mail, fax or phone? Obtain the name of the person to whom you should submit your proposal, along with the correct phone number or e-mail address.

✓ **Meet submission deadlines.** Most TV stations need six to eight weeks' notice. If your big event occurs in April, you need to inform the TV station by February. If it's a human interest story in progress, contact them immediately.

✓ **Get programming guidelines.** What type of project does the TV station accept? For example, some channels offer free exposure to nonprofit entities. Others broadcast only community-related events or qualifying activities such as performances or fundraising events. Still others look for emotionally charged human interest stories.

✓ **Use the community calendar.** These calendars appear as text on the screen, accompanied by an announcer's voice. It is relatively easy to get your event or recruiting activity included here. Put all the details in writing; include a publish-by date and your name as a contact.

✓ **Watch the station.** Analyze public service segments to learn what catches a programming manager's attention. Note time of day programs air and what they feature.

✓ **Be innovative.** Every organization has newsworthy clients or employees or an inspiring goal. For example: "80-year-old twins volunteer at Literacy Center" or "Donated hours exceed 20,000 for the first time in Nature Center's history" or "He once drove an army tank. Now he drives a Meals-on-Wheels van."

✓ **Be persistent.** As one station manager put it, "Submit everything you think our audience would be interested in. The squeaky wheel will eventually get greased. If we see your proposals enough times, we'll probably get around to doing a story on you."

✓ **Show appreciation.** If you do land a TV spot, request a copy. Be sure you follow up with a thank-you note — not an e-mail but a handwritten note. So few people do this that you will be remembered fondly the next time you have a hot piece of news.

Basics of Nonprofit Publicity

Research Media Buyers to Know Their Worth

Media buyers — professionals who are responsible for purchasing media space and time to maximize your message at a minimum cost — can make or break your campaign.

Jeanne Charters, Charters Marketing (Asheville, NC), who spent years doing the buying for several local chapters of a national nonprofit, advises organizations considering investing in a media buyer to:

- ❑ Ask for references. Get a list of people and contact information for those clients they are currently working with or have worked with in the past. Contact each person on the list and ask any who are no longer working with the buyer why that is the case.

- ❑ Ask if the buyer subscribes to Nielsen and Arbitron. Ask them to explain their quantitative and qualitative methods for choosing programs.

- ❑ Ask what their target cost-per-point is in news programming. Just make sure not to ask for a target cost per point for all dayparts since each one varies. Charters says that's a sure way to make you look ignorant to the buyer.

In the end, Charters says it's important to trust your instincts when meeting the person with whom you will hopefully share a long-term relationship. "If there's a shred of arrogance in a media buyer, walk away because some media buyers consider their position a power trip. Any media buyer worth their salt in today's competitive world will be ethical while still looking to maximize your clout at a reasonable price," says Charters. "They should be prepared to seek out value-added elements to most buys, particularly in the non-profit arena."

Source: Jeanne Charters, Charters Marketing, Asheville, NC. Phone (828) 628-0023.
E-mail: jcharters@bellsouth.net

Insider Tip for Using a Media Buyer

Jeanne Charters of Charters Marketing (Asheville, NC), longtime media buyer, offers an insiders' tip for organizations considering using a media buyer:

The changing face of television news can really change your bottom line. Specify that your media buyer ask for the cost-per-point objective in early evening news (6 or 6:30 p.m.). With so many news programs on now, morning, noon and late night would be quite different than early evening.

Gain Media Attention Through Website Links to Current News

Recognizing opportunities to make your organization newsworthy is a matter of luck and diligence. To make both for you:

- ❑ **Stay aware of where your constituents are, and what they're doing, in the overall scheme of news.** When the volcano erupted in Iceland earlier this year, many travelers were stranded overseas. This international event — combined with the ready availability of image transfer through cell phones and other technology — provided the perfect opportunity for many nonprofits to share on-scene reports from students, alumni, or other supporters impacted by this major happening.

- ❑ **Keep up with causes admired people support.** First Lady Michelle Obama focuses on children's health and the well-being of military families. CNN holds an annual Everyday Heroes gala honoring citizens who give generously of their time to many causes. Your volunteers and staff may be involved in spotlight issues because famous people have helped put them there. See what you can do to promote those helping locally.

- ❑ **Be aware of pop culture while spreading good news.** Your independent retirement community's own version of Betty White is celebrating her 80th birthday by doing stand-up comedy at a party for residents. Local media will want to see what this energetic lady has to say about the fulfilling life she leads in your facility.

- ❑ **Check most popular searches online.** Most search engines regularly display the most popular topics users are researching. Study these as a good barometer of hot national issues. Look for the link between current interests and your services for a potential story or lead for your news release.

- ❑ **Be helpful community citizens.** An ice storm paralyzes your city. Nobody cares about any other story. This is the time for your organization to serve in its fullest capacity with manpower, food and water, or a combination of resources. While nobody can eclipse stories of Mother Nature's wrath, you can become a positive part of the coverage. The effects may linger long after order is restored.

Basics of Nonprofit Publicity: Winning Strategies for News Releases, Press Conferences and Media Relations. Edited by Scott C. Stevenson.
© 2011 Stevenson, Inc. Published 2011 by Stevenson, Inc.

Basics of Nonprofit Publicity

News outlets can seem cold and intimidating, but don't let that fool you. Behind the anonymous façade of "the media" are countless writers, reporters, editors and newscasters, each of whom holds the potential for becoming a trusted partner and even friend. Connecting with these flesh-and-blood contacts is key to building working relationships that can benefit both sides for years to come.

Become a Resource for Journalists

Media attention is an invaluable way to raise awareness about your organization, at little to no expense. That is the primary concern of the media relations team at Florida Hospital (Orlando, FL), where they not only give top priority to providing journalists easy access to information about their organization, they have also taken steps to become a resource hub for news in their field.

One way the media relations team does so is through a dedicated presence on the hospital's website filled with resources for journalists and news organizations.

The organization's Media Relations Web page features two parts: 1) readily available media resources including press releases, fact sheets, photos, and video highlighting hospital facilities, projects, programs, staff and news, and 2) three new feeds: Florida Hospital in the News, which features news stories about their hospital as written by outside sources; Health Care Related News, which features the latest health news from outside sources; and Medical Association News, which provides links to organizations like the National Institute of Health and the American Medical Association.

How did the media relations team create this useful resource for journalists?

When it came time to redesign Florida Hospital's media relations website, the media relations team — many of them former journalists themselves — wanted the page to be a one-stop-shop for journalists, says Jennifer Roberts, media relations manager. "It lends a credibility to what we do, as part of the medical community," says Roberts. "The goal was never really to look at numbers — how to drive up hits, so much as it was to aid journalists. Even if the same people are going to the site and getting what they need from it, that's a win for us."

She says the website page's outside news feeds were added as another way to provide an easy user experience for journalists visiting the site.

The entire media relations team participates in maintaining the site; each staffer has access to upload releases, photos and videos. Roberts says staffers stay in constant contact with media outlets, e-mailing and calling journalists and pitching stories. "It's definitely hands-on. With a little training we're all able to get in there and do our part."

While Florida Hospital has a full-time staff devoted to media relations, Roberts says any organization, regardless of size, can easily set up a media hub on its website for little cost, helping to give journalists the resources they need to spotlight your organization in print and on the air.

Source: Jennifer Roberts, Media Relations Manager, Florida Hospital, Orlando, FL. Phone (407) 303-8217.
E-mail: jennifer.n.roberts@flhosp.org.
Website: www.floridahospitalnews.com

Gain Reporters' Respect

Earning the respect of local reporters and media representatives is the most effective way to help ensure a positive working relationship when your organization is the focus of media attention, solicited or not. These five steps will help you build good will with the press corps:

1. **Target your press releases**. Be sure you are sending your news to the correct person, not just the most visible reporter, program host or anchor. The section editor who is most likely to give you ink may not take you seriously as a professional if you haven't bothered to learn his or her name.

2. **Avoid playing favorites with major news**. While it's appropriate to funnel special interest news to reporters who cover that topic (business, social or metro), give competing media equal access to interviews or events for important general interest stories.

3. **Follow up on phone calls and promises**. If you don't

have answers to difficult or controversial questions during an interview, admit that you must investigate further and will call them back before deadline with more details or information. Keep your word and call with an answer or status update, even if it's, "still checking."

4. **Treat media representatives well**. If they are covering a lunch or dinner event, provide meals. Weekend evening events may include a ticket for a guest or spouse. Be sure they are taken care of when they work outside normal business hours and on occasions when everyone is eating.

5. **Build trust with candor about potentially difficult situations**. There may be many reasons reporters should avoid photographing or interviewing some individuals associated with your organization. Give them helpful leads and make appropriate introductions to help them get the best possible story.

Prepare Staff to Interact With the Media

While you likely have a designated media spokesperson, be sure to also take steps to keep other key players in your organization well-versed in what's happening so they are able to respond appropriately, if needed.

Here are four steps to ready those people for their moment in the spotlight:

1. Keep media points up-to-date and make sure all staff, board members and key volunteers get fresh copies when points change. Circulate points by e-mail with a reminder to replace any existing copies with the newest edition.

2. Do a brief media in-service for new staff and board members, briefly instructing them on key issues, words or phrases not to use and media hot buttons — past or present. Educate them on the chain of command to deal with media inquiries and proper response if approached.

3. Keep staff, board members and key volunteers informed of any potential media crises and how to respond to media inquiries on the topics.

4. Keep people updated on positive media coverage. Nothing is worse than receiving a compliment on "the great story in the Gazette," and responding with a blank look. This step helps raise awareness about the work you do among these key players, as well.

Press Release Follow Up — Keep It Personal

You have e-mailed your press release to media outlets. Now what?

Joan Stewart, a media relations consultant and author of the online newsletter *The Publicity Hound* (Port Washington, WI), says, "A press release follow-up cannot be generic, it has to be customized and offer the media outlet something extra."

According to Stewart, too many organizations send out cookie-cutter press releases. Then they make a run-of-the-mill phone call to check and see if it arrived. That kind of follow-up call can actually hurt your chances of getting coverage in the long run, she says, because it makes the media representative feel as if you are wasting his/her time.

So how do you effectively follow up when you send a press release?

First, Stewart says, understand that a press release must be sent to a person and not a department. One to two days after you mail, fax or e-mail your press release, follow up with that specifically designated recipient. Whether you send an e-mail or make a phone call, what you should not do is ask, "Did you get my press release?" Instead try, "I sent you some information, and I wanted to see if you needed anything else." That approach, the media expert says, makes reporters feel important and allows you a chance to bring up some extras that will pique their interest.

To further engage your media contact and increase the possibility of positive media coverage, Stewart says, offer suggestions for a photo or video to accompany the story, and information on an idea for a side story or website link. For newspaper sources, for example, offer an easy-to-read Top 10 list of information related to the topic. For a TV or radio station, provide a website link to more information to further inform the audience and connect them to your cause.

The suggestions you pitch in a follow-up call should be customized for each media contact based on the media venue's core audience. For television and newspapers think people and visuals, Stewart says, "Give them a character."

Take the example of a press release for a fundraising dinner. Without proper follow-up it could get overlooked in a lot of newsrooms. However, when you call the reporter try something like, "Did I tell you about the 87-year-old we are honoring at the event? She's been volunteering for 37 years." The reporter will hear the potential for a story in that character versus just being asked to come and cover the event.

Source: Joan Stewart, Media Relations Consultant & Author, The Publicity Hound, Port Washington, WI. Phone (262)284-7451. E-mail: jstewart@publicityhound.com. Website: http://www.PublicityHound.com. Blog: http://www.PublicityHound.net

Three Press Release Rules You Can't Break

When drafting your press release, you can tap into a variety of formats and styles. While maintaining your individuality and creativity, realize there are a few rules you should not break when writing a press release, says Joan Stewart, media consultant. These include:

1. **No hype** – People don't want to read a press release that is loaded with hype. If you want a commercial, buy an ad. To get their attention, tell them something interesting like how you can help them solve a problem.

2. **Watch the language** – Avoid using words like spectacular, cutting-edge or one-of-a-kind. They are a dead giveaway that your press release isn't really news.

3. **Know your audience** – Unless you are writing for people in your own industry, avoid industry jargon that the public will not understand.

For additional tips on press releases, check out Stewart's free online tutorial session at http://www.89pressreleasetips.com.

How to Host a Media Reception

Looking to boost the media's awareness of your organization? Consider hosting a media reception. Here's how:

- ❑ **Know why you're doing it.** What do you hope to get out of the reception? What would you like the media to do for you? Include that in your call to action (e.g., "Meet three families who overcame serious debt issues, thanks to our consumer counseling service." or "Meet our new CEO and hear her dreams for our cause for 2012.")
- ❑ **Schedule it right.** Host it on what is considered a slow news day and convenient time in your market (e.g., lunchtime won't work for markets with a noon newscast). Ask reporters with whom you are acquainted what time and day they feel would work best.
- ❑ **Keep it brief.** Reporters are busy. Let them know up front how long they can expect to be there. Aim for 30 minutes or less.
- ❑ **Have a plan.** Start on time and offer refreshments. Have your board president or CEO briefly welcome everyone and introduce the key players. Beforehand, instruct that person to keep comments to 10 or 15 minutes. Allow five or 10 minutes for questions, then close with a call to action.
- ❑ **Be prepared.** Have media kits, business cards and extra literature on hand. Prepare a one-pager with a few leads on stories on your cause. Add a calendar of events.

Offer Informal Alternative To the Media Reception

Don't think a formal media reception is right for you or for the particular event you are promoting? Hold an informal media drop-in instead.

Set aside a two- or three-hour block of time when reporters can stop by your office and speak one-on-one with the appropriate people (e.g., those who have benefited from your services, major donors you are recognizing, the architect of your new addition, etc.). Have multiple interview sources available so no one has to wait. Set aside several quiet locations within your facility where people can talk and keep in mind appropriate backdrops for photos or video shoots.

Create Positive Relationship With Local Newspapers

Building a good relationship with your local newspaper can help you reach more of your community and ensure most of your events will be covered. But before approaching publishers and editors for help, know what you can offer in return by:

- ❑ Doing your homework on the newspaper. This means more than subscribing and reading the sports and living sections. Get familiar with the types of stories that make the front page. Study editorials for insight on the paper's perspective on politics, local issues and elected leaders. Are you usually on the same wavelength?
- ❑ Using a courteous, low-key approach. The publisher has agreed to listen to your ideas for spreading the word about your valuable work. Make your case without appearing entitled to lavish praise. Other deserving institutions seek the same attention you plan to solicit. Point out a variety of ways you fill a unique community need, operate with minimal overhead and responsibly use donor funds.
- ❑ Inviting the editorial board to your facility. Allow them free access to department heads, service areas, volunteers, patients or clients to investigate your merits without interference or pressure. Meet with them afterwards for their evaluation and impressions. Encourage them to offer suggestions for improvement. They may find positive stories and human interest features that you never considered.
- ❑ Investigating your newspaper's weak links. Are they losing subscribers to online editions? Not responding quickly enough to new methods of delivering information? Look for areas where they may need help, and see if your organization can help them get up to speed. An equal partnership is usually the most satisfactory.

Build Relationship With Media

Take time to build relationships with local reporters and media representatives. Here are some simple steps for doing so:

- Send handwritten thank-you cards to editors and reporters when you receive positive news coverage.
- Mail local media organizations your newsletter. Good reporters will recognize feature material.
- Give reporters several story ideas and contact names. For instance, do you have a grandmother-son-granddaughter volunteer team? Reporters may follow up on slow news days.
- Invite reporters to help with events such as contests or award presentations. They will often use the invitation to do a story.
- Make yourself immediately available when reporters contact you, being respectful of their deadlines.

Outreach Strategies for Rural-based Nonprofits

If your organization makes its home in a rural setting, your geographic location may restrict you to a more narrow constituency, but you also have the benefit of a captive audience.

Here are some public relations techniques useful to small-town nonprofits:

1. **Forge a positive relationship with the local media.** Because newspaper editors and radio news directors are more accessible than in larger cities, work to educate them on the programs of your organization and build a mutually beneficial relationship. Smaller community media outlets are continually seeking news and feature stories.

2. **Write your own news stories.** Since rural newspapers tend to have few reporters, editors will appreciate news that is already well-written. Editors may print exactly what you send. Experience and the benefit of a close, comfortable relationship will help you pinpoint their preferences.

3. **Make connections with neighboring communities.** Reach beyond your local community by identifying human interest stories with neighboring community connections.

4. **Be a visible member of your community.** Your presence and involvement is much more noticeable and appreciated in smaller communities than larger ones. Your organization's employee involvement in local affairs is also perceived as an important benefit to local residents and community leaders.

5. **Involve media representatives in advisory capacities.** Appoint local editors, reporters and news directors to appropriate committees. Seek input on ways to attract regional and statewide attention.

Three Rules for Managing Your Media Database

Chances are you have a separate database of media outlets to which you can direct news releases and other important information.

Three essential rules for managing that database:

1. **Keep your list current.** Update contact information at least quarterly. Many media outlets have high turnover, and reporters, editors and others are constantly being shuffled.

2. **Make your list segmentable,** allowing you to direct communications to targeted groups. Select only those media outlets that attract the audiences you want to reach.

3. **Learn and adhere to communications preferences.** Learn how different media outlets prefer to receive information (e.g., letter, phone, fax, videotape or e-mail).

Effective Media Databases Require Ongoing Maintenance

A key component of any media relations strategy is a well-managed media database. It is a one-stop shop for contacts you need to attract valuable press coverage.

However, a media database only works for you if you put work into it.

"A media database should contain detailed contact information, including e-mail and mailing addresses, as well as preferred contact method," says Heidi Sullivan, vice president of media research for Cision (Chicago, IL), provider of media relations software services for public relations professionals.

While your first instinct may be to target reporters, Sullivan says, begin building your list with newsroom decision makers. Those are TV assignment editors and managing editors in newspaper and other print outlets. They are the people who receive your press releases and are in charge of assigning reporters to stories.

Individual reporters should be the second tier of your list.

Many small- to medium-sized nonprofits manage their media database on a Microsoft Excel spreadsheet. If starting from scratch, find all of the media outlets in your area.

"Many journalists and outlets provide information on how they want to be contacted and what their deadlines are right on their website," Sullivan says.

Your research does not end here. According to Sullivan, "A media database is an effective tool in determining what media outlets and journalists are the right fit for a campaign." Note what the journalists are doing in your market. Everyone has a different tone, covers different beats and reports on different types of stories. Identifying outlets and journalists geared toward your organization's target audience will help you pitch stories more effectively.

Keeping the media database updated is an absolute must. As a rule, gather key information on your outlets every six months. If needed, consider subscribing to services, like Cision, which provide updated media lists and profiles for thousands of journalists. Whether large or small, there is no better way to get ignored than to send your story pitch to a contact who no longer works at a particular media outlet.

Source: Heidi Sullivan, Vice President, Media Research, CISION US, INC., Chicago, IL. Phone (312)873-6653. E-mail: Heidi.Sullivan@cision.com.

Basics of Nonprofit Publicity

Media professionals are busy people. Deadlines are tight, editors are demanding and time is always of the essence. Comprehensive, concise and well-planned media kits are therefore a must for every nonprofit looking to share its story. Supplying information media representatives can use in formats they prefer can mean the difference between a front-page feature and back-page afterthought.

Offer a Multimedia Online Press Kit

Q. What is the best way to incorporate video into my online press kit?

"A multimedia press kit is definitely the way to go. It is standard to include promotional clips about your agency, but you should also upload videos that speak to specific customers or volunteers. For instance, a hospital could feature a video to explain a new piece of technology and how it will be used. The video serves the dual purpose of being a resource for a reporter and educational for a patient exploring your site."

— Amy Fisher, Director, Technology & Agriculture, Padilla Speer Beardsley (Minneapolis, MN)

Is Your Media Kit Up to Snuff?

Putting together a polished, top-notch media kit can have positive ramifications, including giving the impression that your nonprofit is larger in scope, reputation, experience and capital than it actually is. Here, for-profit and nonprofit PR pros offer advice on assembling a media kit bound to bring you bigger media placements, visibility and exposure:

"Include something original. Everyone has press clips and a one-pager — what sets your nonprofit apart? A well-designed annual report, a collection of photos and brief success stories or a quote collection from influential figures who support your work will give reviewers something sharp, colorful and dynamic to read. But at the same time, don't stuff your kit with extraneous handouts, pamphlets or cards. Deliver content, not clutter."

— Colleen Flynn, Manager of Communications and Media Relations, LIFT (Washington, D.C.)

"Treat your nonprofit like a business and position your board or management as experts in their particular realm. Part of the media kit must focus on these individuals: their bios and headshots, but also a list of several story ideas and topics they can speak to."

— Samantha Lueder, President, Ant Hill Communications (Atlanta, GA)

"Have a consistent look and style. This means print materials must match each other and your online presence. Too many charities, in order to save money, don't update one or the other, creating confusion for potential donors and clients — and wind up looking unprofessional. You can't be top-notch if your press materials look haphaard."

— Sharon Geltner, Founder, Froogle PR (Boynton Beach, FL)

"Put hard numbers into your releases, maybe even a by-the-numbers box that includes number of people served, number of dogs rescued, trash bags of debris collected, students tutored, etc. Numbers give your story real news value that will carry your story beyond the typical fluff feature."

— Deniene Husted, Senior Consultant, SDR Consulting (Atlanta, GA)

"The best media kits for nonprofits do one thing. They justify why their existence matters to the public, and they find clever ways to do it quickly. Nonprofits tend to talk in their own circles, and unfortunately, it shows. It's important for nonprofits to think beyond their natural audience."

— Philip Chang, Partner, Carbon: Publicity & Strategic Communications for Talent (Chicago, IL)

Build Interactive Online Media Kit

When duplicating your on-paper media kit online, be careful what formats you use, says Kevin Leinbach, founder of Web 3.0 Coaching and Consulting (Annacortes, WA).

"(Your online media kit) shouldn't be a single downloadable PDF or ZIP file," he says. Rather, make it interactive. Provide a link on your website's front page to your online media kit or newsroom.

From that link, he says, "provide links to the key information needed by writers and researchers. Collect your most important contact info on one page, images and artwork on another — but provide separate links for your most recent or popular press releases, clippings and white papers, which deserve their own links."

Source: Kevin Leinbach, Founder, Web 3.0 Coaching and Consulting, Annacortes, WA.
Phone (408) 905-8764.
E-mail: kevin@web3coach.com.
Website: www.web3coach.com

Get More Mileage From Your Press Kit

Preparing media kits when you hold press conferences takes considerable time and effort, but you can extend their usefulness and even shelf life using a few of these tips:

- **Keep presentation simple.** A single binder, folder organizer with pockets or even a custom envelope helps ensure your materials will stay together when reporters are ready to write their stories. Too many pieces can make it cumbersome for most journalists' already crammed files.

- **Include attractive ready-to-use photos.** Some media attending your press conference may send writers but not photographers. Make their jobs easier by providing a high-quality selection for newspapers, TV or radio stations to use or post on their websites.

- **Add a calendar of future events.** Briefly describe each event with purpose, time, date, location, chairpersons and contact information so reporters will know in advance about upcoming newsworthy events and photo opportunities.

- **Offer brochures, newsletters and helpful background materials.** Your press kit may be designed primarily for one event, but most journalists appreciate having additional information beyond the news release you have provided to make their stories more complete. This might include brochures highlighting your recent programs and a copy of your latest newsletter.

- **Highlight your own contact information.** Choosing a folder with a business card slot is worth any minor added expense. If appropriate, prepare a roster of your department heads with their contact numbers and e-mails. Most journalists will save listings they think they may use later.

- **Remember that different media have different needs.** You may have radio, newspaper, online news services and television reporters at your press conference. Provide the basics for each of them, but consider customizing different sets of kits for each medium's needs.

Create and Promote an Online Media Kit

A media kit can be the first line of communication about your organization to the outside world. Staff with the Kansas Health Foundation (Wichita, KS) created an online media kit that offers contact information and important details about their organization.

Chase Willhite, communication officer at Kansas Health Foundation, answers our questions about the organization's online media kit:

Why is a media kit important for a nonprofit organization?

"In today's fast-paced business environment, it is important that all constituencies — including media, partners, grantees and the public — are able to quickly access valuable information about our organization. From a media lens, if a reporter just needs some background about our organization, the online media kit allows that person to find basic facts.... If a reporter acquires all the needed information from the media kit, great. If an interview is needed, the background information the reporter now has will, hopefully, lead to a richer, more productive conversation. Additionally, organizations should focus attention on any avenue for increased transparency dealing with organizational facts and information."

What are the most important components of the media kit?

"As with most of our publications, resources or communication strategies, the media kit is designed to answer the questions, 'Who are we?' and 'What do we do?' Our website, in its entirety, provides a wealth of information on our grant making, our history and other points of interest. The media kit, though, provides a quick reference for answering those questions, and potentially leading the reader to explore more about our organization throughout the website. As far as specific components, we include management team information, with links to staff biography pages, contact information, mission, a brief history and an overview of our focus areas as well as funding priorities."

What specific tips do you have for completing a streamlined media kit?

1. "Ask yourself, 'What are the most important elements of our organization we'd like the public to know?'

2. "Make sure the entire online page can be read and digested quickly, while still providing the needed information.

3. "Use a short paragraph or bullet-point format to make the information easier to read.

4. "Offer concise details."

Source: Chase Willhite, Communication Officer, Kansas Health Foundation, Wichita, KS. Phone (316) 262-7676.
E-mail: cwillhite@khf.org. Website: www.kansashealth.org

Online Press Kits Simplify Reporters' Jobs, Increase Interest

If journalists find your website difficult to navigate, they may move on and you may miss out on media coverage.

Solve that problem with an online press kit.

Design your online press kit with the media in mind, says Amy Fisher, director of technology and agribusiness at public relations agency Padilla Speer Beardsley (Minneapolis, MN). "Your online press kit should not just be a collection of things you can find other places," she says. "It should contain things that are specific to the needs of the press."

Offer story ideas on your Web page, including names and contact information for people in your organization to be interviewed on the story topics, Fisher says. Add multi-media elements a reporter can use in the story (e.g., short quotes from board members, images and video clips).

Don't overdo your online press kit. Stick to a couple of key messages. Press releases, for instance, don't belong in an online press kit. They belong with the overall website. Provide a link to them from your online kit.

Finally, Fisher says, know that online press kits can be static to represent your overall organization, or event-specific, made available for a limited duration.

Source: Amy Fisher, Director of Technology and Agribusiness, Padilla Speer Beardsley, Minneapolis, MN. Phone (612) 455-1733. E-mail: afisher@psbpr.com

---

Online Press Kit Samples

Amy Fisher of the public relations agency Padilla Speer Beardsley (Minneapolis, MN) shares links for online press kits her firm has worked on recently:

❑ BASF Professional Pest Control (www. pestcontrolfacts.org/media/) — Basic information media need and links to topic experts on the Contact Us page.

❑ Mayo Clinic Health Manager (http://pub.psbpr. com/microsoft_mayo/CDMediaKit/mediakit. html) — Designed to launch Mayo Clinic Health Manager, this site includes a fact sheet and FAQ for information on the new service, plus a consumer tip sheet with an example of content media could repurpose.

❑ Automation Fair (http://pub.psbpr.com/ Rockwell/AutomationFair2007MediaKit/ mediakit_af.html) —This event-based press site includes a link for media to provide event feedback, event agendas and background materials on products media would see at the event.

Properly Stock Your Press Conference Toolkit

You've sent your news releases and the big day has arrived. Do you have what you need to make the event a success?

Follow this checklist and you will.

❑ **Press packets** including a copy of your news release, a list of who will be speaking with their contact information and correct spelling of their names, a general brochure or fact sheet about your organization and a style guide about writing for your organization.

❑ **Extra copies of news releases** for reporters who don't want to bother with a whole packet of info. Having a few extra releases to hand off to them will prevent you from having to sort through the packets to pull one out.

❑ **Business cards** to give to people for follow-up.

❑ **An attendee sign-in sheet** to help you follow up with attendees.

❑ **A greeter** to welcome people as they arrive, ask them to

fill out the sign-in sheet and hand them a press packet, freeing you to answer questions and mingle.

❑ **Technical support**, or the person who knows how to use the microphone, laptop or other equipment necessary for the conference to go off without a hitch.

❑ **Key constituents** who commit their time or money to you, plus a few people who have benefited from your services. Clarify their roles for them and limit the number you invite, so it doesn't get overwhelming for attendees.

❑ **Light refreshments** that encourage people to linger and get more information after the formal program.

❑ **Miscellaneous needs,** such as tissues, gum, mints, extra pens, note pads, etc. to address those just-in-case emergencies.

❑ **Additional literature** to be taken by any interested attendee.

Update Media Points to Boost Response Time, Accuracy

Ever wonder where a reporter got information about your organization? Want to make sure information reported about your organization is always accurate?

Media points can help.

A quick one-pager listing updated statistical and financial information about your organization can streamline the interview and submission process.

What to include: Current factual and statistical information, including number of people served in the prior year, demographic makeup of those served, number of volunteers, number of board members, cents per dollar raised used towards program services, etc. Include mission statement,

eligibility information, purpose statement (if applicable), number of years in operation and recent milestones.

When to use: Include this versatile document in media kits, with press releases, when being interviewed and in your online pressroom to give reporters a resource, and broadcast reporters and anchors accurate talking points.

Of course, it goes without saying that media points should always be up-to-date. When any change is made, e-mail the updated version to staff, board members and pertinent volunteers, asking them to keep the current version and replace any prior versions.

Understanding Media Guides

A media guide can be a useful tool for your nonprofit.

Creating a media guide, available at your website, can lead media personnel on a path to finding accurate information and the appropriate contacts within your organization to speak with when researching articles. Working with the media, by providing a media guide to your organization, will ensure that the appropriate channels are explored and accurate information is disseminated about your organization.

What is a media guide?

A media guide is a press kit made available online or in print to members of the media featuring information about an individual or organization, history of the organization and contact information.

When is a media guide needed?

All organizations and nonprofits, both small and large, can benefit from gathering the components to compile a media guide. The information contained within the media guide will enable media professionals to find out relevant newsworthy information about the organization and the contacts within the nonprofit to whom they can direct their questions.

What are the primary contents of a media guide?

- Background/historic information. Start compiling your media guide by gathering detailed historic information about your nonprofit outlining the background, growth and goals of the organization.

- Product and service details. List all the services provided by your organization, departments and department contacts including name, e-mail and phone number of the individual listed.

- Recent articles that have been published that highlight the work done by your nonprofit.

- Include current press releases. Be sure to include current press releases that have been distributed by your nonprofit. These documents can alert media professionals to relevant newsworthy topics they can pursue for the publication for which they write. By aiding the press with a media kit, your organization can benefit by receiving notice in the press.

Basics of Nonprofit Publicity

SUCCESSFULLY NAVIGATING INTERVIEWS AND PRESS CONFERENCES

Interviews and press conferences can be a great source of media exposure, but they carry risks as well. Where other forms of publicity can be planned in advance, interviews and conferences involve unscripted and sometimes hard-hitting questions. Knowing how to handle controversial issues, recover from missteps and buy a few seconds to formulate a response will help you put your organization's best foot forward.

When Media Ask, Be Ready To Answer Tough Questions

Picture this: Something is going down within your organization — maybe a staff member was arrested or a volunteer skipped town with some donations. Maybe a client is complaining very loudly and publicly about being turned away.

Now the local media wants answers. How to respond?

Consider the following tips when faced with the tough questions:

✓ Don't feel the need to respond immediately, but do respond. Until you have a chance to be briefed about the circumstances, let calls go in to voice mail or create a reason for a return call. A polite, "I'm on the road. Can I return your call in fifteen minutes?" should suffice. Then, follow through with that return call.

✓ Get up to speed as quickly as possible. While it's OK to defer questions briefly, people will begin to speculate the more time that goes by, which is seldom a good thing. Get the information you need, then move forward.

✓ Only answer what you are asked. Do not offer extra information. Listen to what the reporter is asking and don't be afraid to clarify before responding. Keep your answers as brief as possible and stay on point.

✓ Consider offering an exclusive to an outlet that has been friendly to you in the past. If there's a station or paper that has been supportive, consider offering them an exclusive about the situation in question. For example, if someone on the inside of your organization is accused of embezzling funds, offer your vice president of finance or your board treasurer to the news media. Brief him/her on how to answer questions about how funds are handled, how they are used, what internal and external checks you have in place and how you will be reviewing and/or changing them to prevent similar situations.

Three Ways to Make Any Interview Great

Media Relations Specialist Ginger Daril, Arkansas Children's Hospital (Little Rock, AR), is responsible for planning and coordinating at least 52 television interviews a year. As a result, she knows what makes interviews work. Here are some of her best tips:

1. Provide questions ahead of time so interviewees know what to expect, and ask them more than once. Usually the second time around, the interviewee is more relaxed and can relay the information more comfortably and more succinctly.

2. Throw out a few unscripted questions, which will be strictly conversational, because they didn't prepare responses beforehand. These questions should be things they will know the answer to — with no need for research.

3. Engage with your interviewees, so they forget they are being taped. You can do this by being interested in what they're telling you and letting your facial expressions show your interest. Says Daril, "Sometimes this takes more time than just getting in there, asking the questions and being done — but it makes interviewees more comfortable and ultimately improves the end product."

Source: Ginger Daril, Senior Media Relations Specialist, Arkansas Children's Hospital, Little Rock, AR. Phone (501) 364-1100. E-mail: DarilGL@archildrens.org

Clinch That Radio Interview

If your nonprofit has news to share, seek out interviews with your local radio stations to spread the word. Follow these tips to project a strong, professional presence for your radio interview:

• Listen to the station prior to the interview. Particularly get a feel for the radio personality who will be interviewing you to get an idea of the nature of the show.

• Educate yourself on the type of station where you'll be interviewed. Learn more about the station's demographics and get details on how long the interview will last.

• Practice, practice, practice. Have a friend or colleague prepare a list of questions you'll likely be asked in the interview and practice your responses. Tape the mock interview, so you can work on inflections and information you would like to convey.

• Prepare brief and concise statements and memorize them. Create a 5x7-inch card that contains bullet points of key information about your event or news to use as a reference during the interview.

Take a Step Back to Buy Time Without Turning Off Media

So you're in the middle of an interview and you realize you just said something you wish you hadn't. Maybe you didn't phrase something as well as you could have, or you erroneously gave a wrong fact or bit of information.

How do you correct yourself without coming off badly to the interviewer?

Try saying, "Let me take a step back for a minute." Then give yourself at least a minute to organize your thoughts. This positions you as someone who is being thoughtful about the interview process, rather than someone who just flubbed something.

Feel free to readdress the issue at the end of the interview as well. When asked if there's anything final you'd like to add, say, "I'd just like to clarify that point from before," then reiterate the correct wording or position your organization holds.

Interview Smart

- When a reporter calls unexpectedly with tough questions, understand that you're not obligated to respond immediately. Instead, offer to call back in 10 minutes, giving yourself time to think through an appropriate response.

How to Attract a Press Conference Crowd

Putting together a press conference can be daunting. Even more nerve-wracking is wondering whether anyone will show up for the big event.

The trick to rounding up reporters is to think like one, says Keith Lawrence, director of media relations, Office of News & Communications, Duke University (Durham, NC).

For starters, that means being very selective about whom you invite to your press conference, says Lawrence. A good reporter knows who can always be relied on for a quick quote, as opposed to plum sources who should only be tapped for a major story.

Likewise, you should know which members of the local media like to come out to pressers more than others, and for what topics. General-assignment reporters might be more likely to grab onto any lead, while a beat reporter will only want to be invited when missing it might mean getting scooped by another news outlet. Reporters who are tied to their desks all day long may just appreciate the chance to get out of the office. (How can you find out which kinds you're dealing with? Good, old-fashioned gumshoeing: Call and ask!)

In other words, don't just hit send all on your e-mail every time you're sending out an alert, says Lawrence. "(Journalists) are only going to cover you so many times, so make sure you pick your spots carefully."

Seasoned reporters cultivate and groom sources over many years in order to gain their trust and ultimately get the most important information out of them (think of Deep Throat's involvement in the Watergate scandal). Press-conference management is also relationship-building, he says.

"Journalists will remember if you have called them to something that turns out to be a snoozer," says Lawrence. "On the flip side, if journalists trust you because you haven't led them astray in the past, they're more likely to attend when you do call a press conference."

Once a reporter shows up, your job is to provide all the information he/she needs to put together the story, says Lawrence, "Make sure all the right people are there to answer any questions that may come up." When prepping your presser, do as many journalists do and think around the story from all angles. What questions come up in your mind, and who are the best people from your organization to answer them?

Also remember that different media outlets have different needs — especially TV news, says Lawrence. "If you are inviting TV, make sure there is something visual for them to film," Lawrence says, "and hold the press conference in the late morning or early afternoon, which are times typically convenient for TV news."

Source: Keith Lawrence, Director of Media Relations, Duke Office of News & Communications, Durham, NC. Phone (919) 681-8059. E-mail: keith.lawrence@duke.edu. Website: www.dukenews.duke.edu

News Release Opportunities

What might justify preparing a news release for your organization? Develop a list of justifiable reasons for distributing news releases that includes these and other examples:

- Appointing new employees.
- Launching a new program or service.
- Collaborating with another nonprofit on a program or event.
- Achieving a milestone: most people served, an anniversary and more.
- Bestowing honors or awards on deserving people or organizations.
- Kicking off or ending a fundraising campaign.
- Opening a satellite office or branch.
- Forming partnerships with businesses and other organizations.
- Adding new volunteers.
- Announcing or hosting an event.
- Changing your name or services.
- Honoring long-time employees.
- Citing an achievement of someone served by your organization (student, youth).
- Announcing new board members.
- Completing research.
- Publicizing a major gift or grant.
- Citing an employee's achievement.

Crisis Communication: Practice Makes Perfect

Do you get overwhelmed or intimidated at the thought of planning for communicating in a crisis? You needn't do so, says TJ Walker, media coach with Media Training Worldwide (New York, NY). "Crisis communications interviews are really the same as dealing with journalists at any other time," Walker says, "it is just that the stakes are much higher."

What is at stake is not only the reputation of your organization, but also your effectiveness as a leader. Walker says that in order to perform well as a spokesperson during a crisis, you must practice until you are perfect.

Schedule a crisis communication training session in which you create a scenario and put your spokesperson and top executives through a mock press conference. Set up a video camera and tape interviews. In the role of journalists, place people from within the organization to pummel the interview subject with questions, Walker says. "The people you work with know your weaknesses and will make the training more effective."

Review the taped sessions with the participants. Did they answer each question with the core points of the message cultivated by the crisis team? Were the answers positive, short and engaging?

Walker recommends taping eight interview segments with each participant in a one-day crisis communication session. While that may sound excessive, Walker says, "It takes until about the fourth time before they get comfortable with looking at themselves on camera. Until then, they are focused on the fact that they hate their own voice, or that they don't like what they are wearing."

Once you break through those barriers, you can really begin working with them on their performance. "You need to see yourself do it the wrong way before you can understand why you are getting it right."

Source: TJ Walker, CEO, Media Training Worldwide, New York, NY.
Phone (212) 764-4955. E-mail: tj@mediatrainingworldwide.com.
Website: www.mediatrainingworldwide.com.

Content not available in this edition

Craft Your Crisis Communications

When your organization is impacted by a crisis you will be bombarded by media requests.

Take the time now to know what you will say, says TJ Walker, media coach and CEO with Media Training Worldwide (New York, NY). Walker has 25 years experience teaching newsmakers how to craft and deliver their message during a crisis.

Once you invest in creating a crisis communications manual, he says, test it. Set a day aside to put your policies to the test. Involve all of your organization's key players, create a crisis scenario that you share with them and assign them the task of writing a message in response to the crisis.

Walker defines a media message as "something you can say in 30 seconds that includes the three key points you want to convey to your audience."

To get to that point, first brainstorm to determine the four or five most obvious questions that will come up in the interview, plus one or two questions you think will be the hardest to answer. Then stop focusing on the questions, because while you cannot control the questions a journalist will ask, you can and must control your answers.

Walker uses the acronym PAST to help clients create smart and compelling media answers:

"P" stands for positive. While you cannot control the negative things others, like journalists, might be saying about your organization; you do not want to make your detractors' jobs any easier. While formulating your media messages, sort out the ones that are positive from those that contain mixed or negative elements. You can define a problem without being critical of your organization.

"A" reminds you to answer the most basic questions of who, what, when, where, why and how. By supplying answers easily and quickly to the obvious questions, you show the reporter respect while building your own credibility.

"S" is a clue to keep it short. If you're still talking after 30 seconds, you are going beyond three key message points.

"T" is for the three main points of your message. If you try to communicate more than three ideas in an interview, you end up confusing audiences and reporters. Answer all questions briefly and then bridge back to your main three themes. These 3 points will evolve and be different throughout different stages of the crisis.

Choose Quiet Location, Landline to Maximize Phone Interview

Next time a reporter asks for a live phone interview for a radio or television piece, refer to these tips offered by Ryan Warner, host of "Colorado Matters" on KSFR Colorado Public Radio (Centennial, CO). To sound great on the radio, Warner says:

1. **Choose a quiet place.** Go to a conference room or your office and shut your door to block out noise from your co-workers. Be sure to turn off the phone's call-waiting feature. "It interrupts you by temporarily silencing you," Warner says, which is especially detrimental in a live interview where you don't get a do-over.

2. **Use a landline.** Warner says a landline is best and a cordless phone is the worst. "Many of those phones are of terrible quality, and you get a lot of interference." He also advises getting off the speakerphone or headset.

3. **Position yourself for best sound quality — and best wording of your response.** The closer your voice is to the receiver the better sound quality for the final product. As far as the content for the interview, Warner says, "What works in person and works on the phone (are) compelling answers that are conversational and to-the-point."

Source: Ryan Warner, Host , "Colorado Matters," KSFR Colorado Public Radio, Centennial, CO. Phone (303) 871-9191. E-mail: ryanwarner@gmail.com. Website: www.cpr.org

---

Keep Interview Answers Brief

Q. When interviewed by a TV reporter, how long should my answer be?

"You should be able to say everything important to you on a particular subject in 30 seconds or less. If you find that it takes longer than 30 seconds ... you haven't applied enough mental discipline to the editing process. If you're still talking after 30 seconds, you're actually going on to the fourth, fifth or sixth message point — save those for your speeches, not your media interviews."

— TJ Walker, CEO, Media Training Worldwide (New York, NY)

Tips on Delivering Bad News

Nobody wants to announce offices are closing or a popular program is being cut, but sometimes it has to be done.

Kivi Miller, president of Nonprofit Marketing Guide.com and author of "The Nonprofit Marketing Guide: High-Impact, Low-Cost Ways to Build Support for Your Good Cause," shares advice for delivering bad news while inflicting minimal damage to stakeholder relationships.

When sharing bad news, Miller says, "Always be completely honest and transparent. Don't try to cover up or gloss over unpopular aspects of the news. But also be sure to focus on the positive results that will come from the news or event. Find some kind of silver lining and make that the heart of your message.

"Those who are the most impacted or who will have the strongest opinions — board of directors or major donors — should be notified first and well before the news goes public," she says. "Stakeholders who will be heavily affected — the parents of children attending a daycare that will be closing, for example — should also be given plenty of advance notice. One exception is if you are working to find an alternative to offer. Then it's better to wait to have some good news to deliver with the bad."

If you need to acknowledge culpability or guilt, Miller says, have persons who have the ultimate responsibility for resolving the problem do the talking. Have them address not just the incident itself but steps you have taken to prevent similar situations from happening again. Couple long-term solutions to immediate problems.

Lastly, Miller says, when it comes to sharing bad news, "There is a very fine balance between not sharing enough detail and sharing too much. On one side, if you share bad news but don't explain what happened in sufficient detail, people's imaginations will fill in the gaps, and that will almost always be worse than what really happened. On the other side, people don't need a blow-by-blow of who said what when or a rundown of the reactions of every single board member. They just need to know, clearly and succinctly, why something happened, why it won't happen again, and why the organization will be stronger going forward."

Source: Kivi Miller, President, Nonprofit Marketing Guide.com, Lexington, NC. Phone (336) 499-5816. E-mail: Kivi@ecoscribe.com

Avoid These Three On-camera Interview Errors

Dealing publicly with difficult stories is where spokespeople make their biggest on-camera interview blunders.

Jami Goldstein, public relations director for the Ohio Arts Council (Columbus, OH) says the first and biggest mistake is to tell a reporter "no comment." Doing so makes you look like you have something to hide, says Goldstein. You want your message out in your terms. Telling a reporter "no comment" challenges them to keep digging. Always have an answer even if the answer is that you will have to get back to them.

The second mistake to avoid, Goldstein says, is arguing with a reporter.

"Sometimes a reporter will bait you, but you can't fall for it," she says. Doing so will make you and your organization look bad. If your composure is shaken, take a moment to regain control of yourself. If the reporter is misinformed, calmly tell him he has incorrect information, then share the correct information, if appropriate.

Your third mistake is playing favorites. A public relations professional wants to form good working relationships with all local media contacts. If you are perceived as playing favorites, the payback could be ignoring you when you need coverage.

Source: Jami Goldstein, Director, Public Information Office, Ohio Arts Council, Columbus, OH. Phone (614)728-4475. E-mail: jami.goldstein@oac.state.oh.us. Website Resource: http://oac.ohio.gov/resources/ mediaresourceguide/interview.asp

Four Ways to Prep Clients to Shine in Media Spotlight

There is no doubt that the people you serve can and often do make the most compelling case for giving to your organization. Unfortunately, these people may be the least likely to have actually done media interviews before.

But don't let lack of experience prevent you from encouraging and coaching these important spokespersons to do media interviews. Just use these tips to prepare them, and it should be smooth sailing:

❑ **Choose wisely.** If someone tells you he/she isn't comfortable or is shy and reserved, think twice before proceeding. Chances are there are several people you have served who would be eager to speak to the media. Narrow your pool down to them.

❑ **Give parameters.** Let the designated spokespersons know what they should be addressing. Generally they should be speaking about their personal experiences with the organization. Tell them not to worry about the organization's history or clarifying what you do. This should help ease their anxiety, because they don't have to worry about memorizing facts and figures. They will only be speaking about what they know.

❑ **Do a dry run.** Role play the first few times someone is going to be speaking on camera for you — before the big day. This gives you both a chance to work out the kinks. You play the role of reporter and let them know what questions they might expect, then give them the chance to actually answer them.

❑ **Have a backup.** Always have an official spokesperson on standby. In case the interview does not go as planned, the reporter will likely be looking for additional information from someone else. Make sure that someone else is available.

Basics of Nonprofit Publicity: Winning Strategies for News Releases, Press Conferences and Media Relations. Edited by Scott C. Stevenson.
© 2011 Stevenson, Inc. Published 2011 by Stevenson, Inc.

Basics of Nonprofit Publicity

Special events must attract large numbers of participants to be successful, and that means publicity. Community and general-admission events can be a great opportunity to promote an organization, but organizers must plan ahead to make the most of such opportunities. Make sure your outreach generates the exposure your organization needs by mastering a variety of promotional efforts — from social media initiatives and news releases to celebrity involvement and word-of-mouth marketing,

Five Ways to Maximize Major Event Publicity

Some special events impact your organization beyond a mere press release, and you hope to maximize the positive attention they bring. Develop a variety of ways to share the news with different audiences, but in different ways.

1. **Share client Tyestimonials**. Your organization has been named top provider of services in your field by an independent group. Ask some of the most compelling clients you have served to go on camera or on the record for commercials, advertisements and feature stories that you can use at intervals throughout the year.

2. **Spotlight your benefactors**. A longtime supporter has left your institution a bequest that will allow you to build an addition, or ensures continuity of services for years to come. Who is or was this person? Write an article about his or her life, association with your organization and reasons for choosing you for this major gift. Explain how it will positively impact the community.

3. Publicize **first-in-the-region status**. Being first to obtain life-saving equipment, whether at the fire station or in the operating room, is a claim to fame you can enjoy even after competitors have caught up. Develop a brief but descriptive tag line to use on all publications and advertising for as long as it is applicable, or until you have a new first to promote.

4. **Host a celebration activity**. Invite the community to share in your good fortune by holding an open house, family festival or free concert that trumpets your good news while also showing your gratitude. Publicity for the event should center on the reason for the celebration, and result in free media coverage.

5. **Award a scholarship**. Helping a deserving student who has a connection to your organization is an excellent way to express thanks for community support that led to your achievement. Media coverage about the recipient will bounce back to the reason you founded the scholarship in the first place.

Pair Diverse Event Activities To Double Publicity Options

Opposites can attract attendees and media attention to your event. To breathe new life into your annual events that may be growing stagnant, mix in a new and unexpected twist, and watch your possibilities for media coverage grow exponentially.

For example, here are ideas to put a new twist on traditional fundraising events:

❑ **Add an eat-and-run theme to your run/walk.** You know this event always brings in serious local athletes and crowds to cheer them on, but adding a healthy cooking exhibit during and after the race can attract non-athletes and sponsors. Seek out area restaurants, caterers and health food businesses to prepare and share their products with new audiences. For additional entertainment — and potential media coverage — add a healthy cooking contest or cooking challenge, al a Food Network.

❑ **Please everyone's palette by adding comfort foods to your wine auction.** Make your wine auction appealing to a broader base — and more photo and story ideas — by encouraging chefs and sommeliers to join forces for the best combinations of wine and everyday meals like macaroni and cheese, beef stew, chili and cheeseburgers.

❑ **Add fun to your fashion show with a Real House-wives-meet-Thrifty Sisters approach.** Imagine the fun when you can combine the lavish lifestyles of Bravo TV's "Real Housewives" series and the recycled chic of Nate Berkus and the Thrifty Sisters from his popular daytime show. Your next fashion production could showcase ensembles from both upscale boutiques, your supporters' own closets and a mixture of both.

❑ **Pump up the marketing potential with creative combinations in a His and Hers silent auction.** Create sparkling packages with diamond earrings and power washers, and a weekend package that starts with her at a spa and him at a sporting event, then brings them together for a romantic dinner. Add to the contrasting theme of girlie-girl and manly-man items by serving champagne and finger sandwiches alongside burger sliders and beer.

Social Media Campaign Draws Attention to Day of Giving

Christopher Whitlatch, manager of marketing and communications, The Pittsburgh Foundation (Pittsburgh, PA), says many organizations participating in its 2010 Day of Giving developed social media campaigns to promote their participation in the event.

To help nonprofits new to social media get started using it, foundation officials hosted four sold-out workshops and posted webinars on the foundation website.

In September 2010, the foundation launched the Adopt an Organization program that encouraged persons to assist nonprofits in getting the word out about the Day of Giving through Facebook and Twitter posts encouraging others to give to a particular organization.

Throughout the day, Whitlatch says, Twitter and Facebook were abuzz with compliments and updates. Congratulations came from organizations nationwide as they monitored progress on social media. Twitter promoted the foundation on its main page of featured tweets, and the Day of Giving was the top local trend on Twitter for several days.

Source: Christopher Whitlatch, Manager of Marketing and Communications, The Pittsburgh Foundation, Pittsburgh, PA. Phone (412) 394-2620. E-mail: whitlatchc@PGHFDN.ORG

Generate Buzz for Your New Construction Project

As the saying goes, "Any publicity is good publicity." But when it comes to a construction project, is it true?

"Absolutely," says Mike Vietti, communications director for KaBOOM! (Washington, D.C.) a nonprofit organization that coordinates volunteers to build about 200 playgrounds across North America every year. That averages out to one new playground every two days, and, Vietti says, "We publicize each and every one of those projects."

Why should you publicize the construction of a new facility?

"The promotion of the construction of a new facility is an absolute no-brainer for KaBOOM! We use our highly engaging, done-in-a-day volunteer playground builds as a stepping stone to introducing the consumer population to KaBOOM!, supplementing our development efforts to build additional playgrounds and increasing awareness for the unfortunate play deficit that exists throughout the continent. The volunteers also enjoy a massive sense of pride and accomplishment upon returning home from a hard day's work to see the playground they helped build on the evening news or in the newspaper the following day. The construction of any new facility is frequently an exciting occasion, and we deliberately structure our playground builds so that they produce highly visual footage and exceptional story lines for media outlets."

What steps should you take to publicize either the announcement of the construction or the construction of the project itself?

"If you plan on pursuing media for any kind of construction project, you absolutely must take their needs into consideration during the planning process. You need to create an inviting and engaging media opportunity that merits the media's attention. KaBOOM! projects begin with a Design Day in which children spend time drawing their dream playgrounds with those drawings ultimately incorporated into the design for the playgrounds we build eight to 10 weeks later. This is a highly visual and engaging event for media — who wouldn't want to cover a story about children designing their own future playground? This kickoff event also serves as a vehicle for contacting media about the larger playground build down the road — even if they don't cover the KaBOOM! Design Day, we've alerted media about the overall project and securing coverage for the playground build will be easier. Our playground builds involve hundreds of volunteers constructing a child-designed playground in less than eight hours, which is an exceptional event for media coverage."

What are some steps you take to secure coverage?

"The key to securing media coverage for KaBOOM! playground builds is that we've created an event tailor-made for media coverage and for each playground build, we maintain the necessary persistence in pursuing media coverage. KaBOOM! uses standard communications practices for securing coverage (press releases, media advisories, Twitter, Facebook, etc.), but I've found over the years that you cannot rely solely on electronic contact. You need to pick up the phone and call reporters."

Do you share your knowledge with other nonprofit agencies?

"The KaBOOM! structure of our playground Design Day and playground Build Day took years of formulating and adjustments, but even our first build in 1995 received significant media coverage because we took an ordinarily pedestrian event and created a highly visual and engaging project involving hundreds of volunteers from the community. Any organization can replicate this process for a construction event and create the success KaBOOM! has enjoyed during the course of the 1,900-plus playgrounds we've built. We compiled all of the knowledge gained from building playgrounds and packaged it in an accessible format on our website (www.kaboom.org) for free. These step-by-step guides and webinars include instructions for all aspects of a playground build — including public relations, creating media materials and media outreach."

Source: Mike Vietti, Communications Manager, KaBOOM!, Washington, D.C. Phone (202) 464-6076. E-mail: MVietti@kaboom.org. Website: www.kaboom.org

Custom Facebook Pages Boost Event Attendance

Imagine if you could triple attendance at one of your organization's long-standing events. Technology and social media can help make that happen, says Michael Howard, principal, At Your Service Business Consulting (Albany, NY).

Howard says he helped the local chapter of the Leukemia and Lymphoma Society (LLS) use Facebook to increase attendance at its annual Taste of Compassion wine-tasting event from an average of 250 attendees to nearly 650 over two years.

To do so, Howard designed an expanded "mini website" page, known as a custom Facebook page, which allowed more photos and copy, PDF downloads and links to buy tickets.

The Taste of Compassion Facebook page brought people involved with other parts of the organization, such as 1,200 persons involved in a marathon fundraising program, in as fans. Howard says Facebook opened up a huge communications medium with those people — most of whom are younger — about how "cool" the wine tasting event is.

Regular updates on prizes, wineries and ticket sales had a viral effect, leading sponsors and friends of sponsors to become fans.

He says the first year using Facebook saw attendance grow from 250 to 400, necessitating a change in venue. The following year, the event drew 650.

Howard says the custom page also serves as a cross-promotion platform for events throughout the year.

"Fans rarely leave, so it is easy to place a post on the Taste of Compassion page for the spring event, which also has its own Facebook page," he says.

"The LLS chapter has its own page for communication not related to a particular event. All of the organization's pages keep them in communication with their most likely supporters, creating a community among supporters of the organization and allowing them to communicate with each other. This can't be achieved with traditional fundraising mailings and telemarketing campaigns."

Source: Michael Howard, Principal, At Your Service Business Consulting, Albany, NY. Phone (518) 449-2420.
E-mail: mhoward@consider-done.com.
Website: www.consider-done.com

Anatomy of a Post-Event Media Release

A post-event media release is a great way to highlight the results of successful events and further promote your cause, says Melissa Cardenas, development coordinator for the Guild Association, Seattle Children's Hospital (Seattle, WA).

Cardenas offers steps for crafting a winning post-event release:

1. **Title** — This should be a complete sentence (subject and verb) that gets attention, using powerful words such as new, first, last or exclusive.
2. **Lead paragraph** — Start with an attention-grabbing first sentence and include a description of the event or project, answering who, what, when, where, why and how. This paragraph should also answer the question, "Why should people care?"
3. **Recognition** — Thank your event sponsors and name them at the end of the release before the boilerplate.
4. **Boilerplate** — This is a general statement about your organization appropriate to include in any release. It may include your mission statement, whom you serve and any other pertinent details about your organization.

5. **Media contact information** — Whom should the media contact if they are interested and what is the most direct way of doing that? This should include name and contact information for the person responsible for the release, as well as a backup in case that person is not available.

Offering to provide photos can also help improve your chances of your post-event press release seeing print or air time, Cardenas says. However, she doesn't recommend sending photos as an attachment. Rather, use online photo-hosting sites.

"Flickr (www.flickr.com) is a great photo resource, and you can add links to e-mail press releases," she says.

In the end, though, remember that your work should focus on newsworthiness. "There is a lot of news out there. Finding the most unique and interesting elements of your event to highlight can entice the media to write about it."

Source: Melissa Cardenas, Development Coordinator, Guild Association, Seattle Children's Hospital, Seattle, WA.
Phone (206) 987-6806.
E-mail: Melissa.cardenas@seattlechildrens.org

Wrap Up Your Event With Wrap-up Press Release

You've done it all, from pre-planning to hosting to cleanup for your event. Don't forget one important detail: the wrap-up press release.

Although you may feel like kicking back and enjoying the accolades of a job well done, the event is not complete without sending a press release to the media, senior management, sponsors, volunteers and major participants that contains:

- ✓ Official name, date and number of attendees at the event.
- ✓ A heartfelt quote from your president or director about the event's importance.
- ✓ Information on presentations made or awards given, as well as speakers or recipients.
- ✓ Details on how funds were raised, how much was raised and what for, if applicable.
- ✓ Acknowledgement of major donors and sponsors of the event.
- ✓ Staff recognition and volunteer participation with a note of gratitude.
- ✓ Details about next year's event. If not all details are finalized, share information you have, plus contact information on whom to contact to become involved next year.

Four Ways to Promote an Unsuccessful Event

A post-event media release is a great way to spotlight your successes and continue to raise awareness about your organization. But what if your event wasn't that successful, at least from a fundraising perspective? You can still use a post-event release to garner additional attention by focusing on what worked well. Here are four angles to consider:

1. **Sponsor spotlight:** Thank all of your sponsors and feature one or two of the event's major sponsors, highlighting what they do for your organization and specifically how they helped with this particular event.

2. **Milestone:** Did you celebrate a significant milestone in conjunction with the event? If so, pitch the story as a then-and-now piece (e.g., how things have changed since you opened your doors), or focus on the milestone itself.

3. **National trend tie-in:** If your event once raised major funds, but fell short due to the economy's impact on significant supporters and sponsors, use that angle to get a reporter's ear. Talk about the effect the economy has had on your fundraising efforts, using this event as an example. Share ways in which you hope to boost event revenue for your next event, and how local people can help you succeed in doing so.

4. **Testimonial:** Pitch the story of someone who benefited from your services and spoke at the event on your behalf. This human element will draw attention to what is important — the work you do and how fundraising events make that happen.

Track Your Nonprofit's News Coverage

If your media department has been diligently spreading the word about your nonprofit's annual events, one-time events or deeds bettering the community, why not capture that coverage on your website? News coverage about your nonprofit offers power-packed information for your website and adds credibility to your cause.

Follow these tips to capture media coverage:

- ✓ **Capture video streams from local news stations to post on your organization's website.** Visual aides such as these are dynamic and allow interested parties to get the full scope of your organization's purpose.

- ✓ **Scan newspaper articles.** Clip and scan newspaper coverage about events, donations or your organization's philanthropy within the community. Also, scan the front page of the newspaper to capture the date of the coverage. Newspaper coverage is detailed and offers an archival account of the work done by your nonprofit.

- ✓ **Audio stream radio interviews that feature your nonprofit's leaders.** Listeners can hear about your nonprofit's goals straight from the leaders themselves.

- ✓ **Gather press releases that your media staff has created and include them under a press release tab on your website.** This information allows researchers and news writers easy access to the latest information about what new things your organization is doing.

- ✓ **Create a media tab on the main page of your nonprofit's site where you can post all of the above news-related items.** This assists those interested in your organization in staying up-to-date with the latest breaking news from all mediums.

- ✓ **When posting media clips from radio, news or print outlets,** be sure to obtain copyright permission from the source before posting them to your site.

Basics of Nonprofit Publicity

DRAFTING APPROPRIATE POLICIES AND GUIDELINES

Media relations policies, press release policies, crisis response policies though not the most glamorous thing in the world, guidelines like these are crucial to effective public relations strategies. They allow organizations to act on sound principles instead of shifting circumstances, and save leaders from having to reinvent the wheel with every new situation. Make sure your policies have what it takes by considering the advice in the following articles.

Craft Media Guidelines

When officials with Howard University (Washington, D.C.) published their media guidelines as part of their "Graphic and Standards Manual" in 2005, it was the first comprehensive branding strategy the university had unveiled in its history. The guidelines are also part of a more proactive and strategic interaction with the media.

"We needed parameters for what was news, what was worthy of pitching to the external media, etc.," says Kerry-Ann Hamilton, media relations manager. "We have limited resources and personnel; therefore it is critical that we be highly selective and ensure that the stories we advance are consistent with our key messages and the vision priorities outlined by our president and board of trustees."

Hamilton says the guidelines send a more cohesive message by allowing for measurement of outcomes based on the direct result of media pitches against key messages. They also encourage community members to share any possible issues with the university's communications and marketing departments so that staff can be proactive.

Within the guidelines is a policy for considering exceptions, which are considered on a case-by-case basis through arbitration by a branding committee.

While the guidelines are not foolproof, Hamilton says that having early buy-in from the university president, as well as from senior administrators, deans and directors has helped. "Because of their oversight of the respective units, we count on them to orient new faculty and staff to the policy and to reiterate the policy to their direct reports."

Source: Kerry-Ann Hamilton, Media Relations Manager, Howard University, Washington, D.C. Phone (202) 238-2332. E-mail: k_hamilton@howard.edu

Six Must-haves In Your Media Relations Policy

A well-planned media relations policy can save you time and headaches by streamlining the workflow of your communications department and preventing unwanted media access. To make sure yours is up to snuff, Debra Stevens, director of marketing and communications at Phoenix Children's Hospital (Phoenix, AZ), suggests the following:

1. **Adherence with relevant national guidelines.** In the case of a healthcare facility, that means following HIPPA guidelines, as determined by federal law, to protect patients' personal health information. While your organization may not be bound by any federal laws, if you're a local chapter of a national nonprofit organization, the same idea will apply. Learn what best practices, determined from on high, you should uphold.

2. **A single method for handling every media request.** No matter how big or small the media outlet and no matter what the specific nature of the request, all media requests should be handled in exactly the same way. At Phoenix Children's Hospital, Stevens says, that means "requiring all media to first obtain permission from the communications department to conduct an interview," and second, "to accommodate every reasonable media request, providing the highest-ranking content expert as spokesperson." Once you start making exceptions, you start increasing your workload and chances of unwanted media exposure.

3. **Round-the-clock media access to your organization.** At Phoenix Children's Hospital, a simple pager number that is answered 24/7 by a member of the communications department is all that's needed. Depending on the nature of your organization, such constant access may not be necessary. However, this can be a low-cost, low-maintenance way for your group to gain a reputation as a source upon which reporters can always rely.

4. **Posting your policy on your website.** But don't stop there. Stevens also strongly suggests that "the best way to communicate (your) policy is to build strong, positive relationships with members of the media."

5. **Reviewing your policy routinely.** "Most policies are reviewed every two to three years," Stevens says. "Revisions are vetted through a policy committee and, ultimately, reviewed and approved by the board of directors."

6. **Deciding in-house which sources to provide.** A reporter may request to interview a specific member of your organization by name. However, that doesn't mean you can't make it a practice to steer the person toward someone else you see as a better fit for the interview.

Source: Debra Stevens, Director of Marketing and Communications, Phoenix Children's Hospital, Phoenix, AZ. Phone (602) 546-0824. E-mail: dstevens@phoenixchildrens.com. Website: www.phoenixchildrens.com

Why Having a Press Release Policy Is a Must

When you are building a brand, you want a consistent message.

Cody Pinkston, director of media and public relations at Ripon College (Ripon, WI), cites this requirement for consistency as one of the main reasons he implemented a press release policy at the college in Fall 2009.

"Everything that a college-sponsored group sends out to the media is considered to be an official college communication," Pinkston says. "For that reason, certain standards have to be followed."

Since there are numerous groups on campus, Pinkston drew up a press release policy and posted it on Ripon's website as a one-stop shop for every department.

At the heart of the policy is a downloadable press release template that allows users to insert their copy using the fonts and sizes indicated on the template. It keeps the look and feel of all of Ripon's press releases consistent.

Pinkston says the communication department needs to operate as if they are the public relations shop for the college and all of the various departments and groups are their clients. "The policy allows us to help our clients determine what they want, how to put the press release together and then shows them what they can expect from it."

Next, the focus is on education. The policy offers up questions that help the user focus his information for the release. "We need to make sure the departments are including the who, what, when, where and why of an event. We also offer a style guide the departments can use to ensure correct grammar, spelling and style."

Once the press release is written using the template, it is sent to the communications department where it is professionally edited and distributed to news outlets, Pinkston says. "We make sure the departments understand that just because a press release is issued, it is not a guarantee it will get coverage."

Pinkston says there has been a slow-burn response to the press release policy. "It has only been up and running for a few months, so the biggest challenge is breaking the habits of the people who have been doing it their own way for years."

Source: Cody Pinkston, Director of Media and Public Relations, Ripon College, Ripon, WI. Phone (920) 748-8365. E-mail: PinkstonC@ripon.edu. Website: www.ripon.edu

Guidelines Help You Prepare for a PR Crisis

Sexual harassment claims, embezzlement, accidental death or injury of a client while on your premises — the list of possible crisis scenarios for your organization is almost endless. These basic guidelines can help you, as your organization's official spokesperson, prepare to handle crisis situations:

Prepare for crisis from your first day: Some crises may never gain public attention, but reporters may notice anonymous blog chatter or act on tips from organization insiders. Begin cultivating media contacts as soon as you start your new job. Existing relationships will benefit you both when the press expects instant feedback on tough questions.

Have an answer ready for the press: Even if the answer is, "We're still gathering pertinent facts right now," with a promise of more details to come, respond quickly to calls. If pressed, admit that you don't know. Whatever your initial answer, remain consistent until you have a more detailed one.

Coping with litigation: Your organization is sued, and the plaintiff's attorney is holding court with reporters. You are forced to respond and may have to have your own attorney. Let counsel speak for you when possible, but stay in touch with your media contacts. When you are allowed to discuss the case, be forthright about decisions your leadership made, such as declining opportunities to resolve, e.g., "We didn't see the point in using funds for attorneys that could be used for our programs."

Assure donors that their funds are well-used: Let donors know that their money is not being used to fight a lawsuit, but for intended purposes. If appropriate, have a separate legal defense fund where those who desire to help can make donations.

Keep supporters and volunteers up-to-date: Set up an official blog or website link where interested parties can get current facts and developments directly from your organization. Try to make regular entries at set intervals (e.g., once a week) so persons who closely follow developments will know when to check back. This will help avoid confusion that may result from rumors or anonymous bloggers who may have their own agendas.

Consider Confidentiality When Sharing Stories

Federal laws associated with the Health Insurance Portability and Accountability Act (HIPAA) of 1996 make it more challenging to promote stories from a public relations and marketing standpoint, especially for nonprofits in a healthcare setting.

Sue Ann Culp, executive director, Holland Hospital Foundation (Holland, MI), shares one method for doing so:

"Due to very strict HIPAA regulations, some stories have been altered to protect identities and may partially reflect a compilation of two stories. Rarely will people allow their story to be printed with their real picture and details that could identify them. The same message can be given, (even while) interchanging ages, gender and medical conditions. Our constituents understand this practice. They understand that identities have to be protected and do not expect more. The effectiveness remains high, because it still allows donors to personalize the outcome of their gifts and understand the relevance, magnitude and importance of their gift as it relates to real people in our community."

Source: Sue Ann Culp, Executive Director, Holland Hospital Foundation, Holland, MI. Phone (616) 355-3974. E-mail: saculp@hollandhospital.org

Formulate and Publicize Social Media Guidelines

Well-crafted social media guidelines foster openness and encourage growth while establishing what is appropriate for that organization.

Heidi Sullivan, vice president of media research for Cision (Chicago, IL), says, "Whether your organization has committed to a social media presence yet or not, it's now readily apparent that it should establish guidelines that spell out the rules and standards of online engagement and behavior."

Many organizations post social media codes of conduct on their websites. To begin crafting yours, see what others are doing, or start from scratch and create a set of guidelines that reflect the nature and needs of your organization.

Sullivan, who has studied and developed a variety of social media policies, says these are her five best practices.

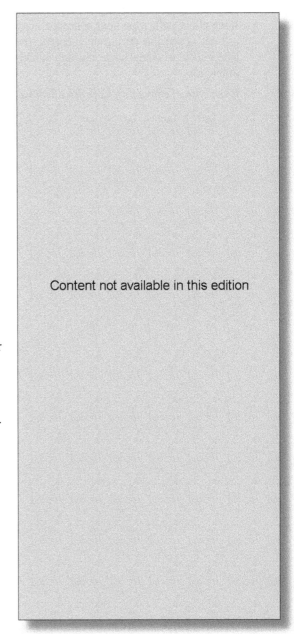

Content not available in this edition

- ❏ **Think like a spokesperson.** Every employee with a Facebook page or Twitter account essentially becomes a spokesperson for your organization. Your policy for employees should include the same limitations and guidelines your official spokesperson has about what they can and can't reveal about the company.

- ❏ **Designate representatives.** For your official social media sites, decide who your representatives are and give them limitations on their personal social media involvement. Other staff can be personally involved with social media but should not identify themselves with your company or brand.

- ❏ **Avoid jargon.** Use language employees and volunteers can understand.

- ❏ **Identify off-limits subjects.** The more specific you are, the easier your policy is to enforce. Do not assume everyone knows what is controversial for your agency.

- ❏ **Open a discussion.** Bring your employees into the planning process.

Finally, Sullivan says, don't forget the word social in social media. Removing personality or opinion from these sites is not possible, and should not be your goal. However, with a little controlled messaging and a few guidelines, you can foster growth through social media without risking embarrassment or worse from an employee or volunteer.

Cision offers a social media guidelines white paper that is available for download at http://us.cision.com/campaigns/2009_sm_policy/request.asp.

Source: Heidi Sullivan, Vice President, Media Research, CISION US, INC., Chicago, IL. Phone (312) 873-6653. E-mail: Heidi.Sullivan@cision.com.

Create Emergency Communications Plan

What is your nonprofit's plan of action in the case of fire, flood, gas leak, hostage situation or other emergency?

Create a plan that details ways you will communicate with your constituents, staff and volunteers in the event of an emergency. Put into play the following tips:

- Determine the best form of communication among your staff and how you will relay emergency information to constituents. Consider text messaging as a form of contact between leaders and staff members.

- Find a simple way to relay information to constituents in the event of an emergency. Consider posting information to your website or via your Facebook page to alert constituents about how the emergency is affecting your agency and service to them.

- Keep phone calls from your nonprofit's main number as brief as possible during an emergency to allow emergency personnel to get through quickly and efficiently.

- If the type of emergency does not allow for communication to and from your facility, create a partnership with a neighboring nonprofit to allow staff and volunteers to communicate from an area of that nonprofit to allow for communication with emergency professionals, staff and/or constituents.

- Keep cell phones charged and a car charger for your phone in your vehicle.

- Maintain a current list of emergency phone numbers for fire, police, staff and volunteers in your office and your main reception area. Program these numbers into your cell phone as well.

- Designate an external meeting location for internal personnel. Develop a plan to get out of the building should there be immediate concern for safety of those onsite. Share this information in staff and volunteer training.

- Post emergency exit information prominently throughout your building.

Basics of Nonprofit Publicity

REACHING OUT THROUGH SOCIAL MEDIA

Traditional media has long been a staple of nonprofit publicity, but more and more people are turning to their computer instead of their television or newspaper for news and entertainment. Social media has revolutionized numerous areas of nonprofit functioning, and publicity is no different. Organizations must be become increasingly adept at reaching out through these platforms, if they wish to remain visible and relevant.

Use Social Media as an Effective Marketing Tool

An important first step in creating effective social media connections is to talk about social media marketing, not just social media, says David Sieg, vice president of strategic marketing at YourMembership.com, Inc. (St. Petersburg, FL). "Social media is a new and quickly evolving trend, but its value lies in very traditional marketing goals like raising revenue and growing membership," Sieg says. "Organizations need to make sure that focus on marketing isn't lost in a sea of fans and tweets."

Here Sieg answers three common questions about social media marketing.

Which social media platforms produce the most consistent results?

"I recommend Twitter as a first focus, followed by LinkedIn and Facebook as a distant third. Services that can augment social media marketing include Flickr for sharing photos, YouTube for sharing videos and organizational blogs."

Where should our blog be hosted — as part of the organizational website or as a stand-alone site?

"We do a lot of work with search engine optimization and have found the best approach to be a WordPress blog installed on your website and hosted internally. This is a free application that is very flexible in look and feel and very good at getting indexed by search engines."

What kind of tone should we use in social media?

"Ironically, one of the biggest mistakes we see is organizations being too social with social media. If your president wants to talk about local sports teams on his or her personal blog, that's fine, but organizational communications need to be focused on conveying useful information and unique insight."

Source: David Sieg, Vice President, Strategic Marketing, YourMembership.com, Inc., St. Petersburg, FL. Phone (727) 827-0046. E-mail: dsieg@yourmembership.com. Website: www.yourmembership.com

Maximize Your Message on Twitter in 140 Characters or Less

A nonprofit's Twitter account can be a gold mine for fundraising, volunteer outreach, marketing and publicity. The trick is figuring out how to best communicate your organization's purpose and needs in Twitspeak.

For example, one rule of Twitter is that each tweet (electronic message to persons who sign up to follow you) can contain no more than 140 characters of type, including punctuation and spaces. So what can you convey in such a short space that can result in a positive change in your organization's bottom line, membership base or press coverage?

Jennifer Roccanti, development associate at Miriam's Kitchen, a Washington, D.C.-based provider of meals and essential services for the homeless, uses Twitter daily.

"We've found that people genuinely want to make a difference in the lives of our guests," says Roccanti, "and Twitter is one way we can connect our supporters to ways they can help." Here are her recommendations for tweeting to your best advantage.

Use recurring headers. Many Miriam's Kitchen tweets begin "One Thing You Can Do Today To Help," and then suggest something inspirational "Give thanks for the people in your life," or ask for something, "Can you spare a warm hat for a person on the street?". Other tweets start with "On the Menu This Morning," listing what Miriam's Kitchen will serve guests that day, allowing people to feel connected to Miriam's Kitchen on a daily basis. But the tweets that generate the most results are those that begin, "On Our Wish List Today." Which is why Roccanti most recommends that you...

Tweet for in-kind donations. More than fundraising, Twitter has proven to be a gold mine for Miriam's Kitchen when in need of specific items. Roccanti might ask for something like, "Men's jeans, especially sizes 34 and 36." "We try to be as specific as possible and mention things that really anyone could do," she says. "We want to give our supporters a quick way to get involved, and they've really responded. In fact, I just got a huge box of books from one of our friends on Twitter."

Get personal. "Our most popular tweets are ones about our guests or the struggles they are facing," says Roccanti. "Statistics about homelessness, stories about our guests or links to articles about the issue at large are usually retweeted." Retweets (when a user forwards your tweets to his or her own followers) are an easy and effective way to expand your potential base of donors and members and to spread your message far and wide — with others doing the work for you.

Jennifer Roccanti, Development Associate, Miriam's Kitchen, Washington, D.C. Phone (202) 452-8926. E-mail: jenn@miriamskitchen.org

Social Networking Creates Community of Followers

Social networking — the use of Twitter, Facebook, LinkedIn and the like — can help build a sense of community among those who believe in your cause.

At Miriam's Kitchen (Washington, D.C.), Jennifer Roccanti, development associate, says they attract followers by publicizing their Twitter and Facebook pages in print, e-mail and online materials.

"We let our supporters know that a great way to keep in touch with us and up-to-date on our programs is through Twitter and Facebook, in the hope that they'll come join in the conversation," she says. "This type of advertising is perhaps most effective for gaining new Facebook followers. We attract new Twitter followers when our existing followers 'retweet' our content or mention us in a tweet."

They track content sharing primarily through Google Alerts searches in Facebook and Twitter for the words, "Miriam's Kitchen."

Roccanti says social media also helps the nonprofit:

- Keep supporters aware of what's happening at the organization and where their money is being spent;
- Show what their guests' successes and struggles look like;
- Share information and resources so that their supporters feel a part of the movement to end homelessness.

Roccanti says she and her co-workers constantly work to balance promotion and engagement through their social networks. "It's important for us to use social media to thank people for volunteering, to wish happy birthdays to our friends and to congratulate people on their accomplishments," she says. "It's hard to balance all of that and still keep our information interesting and relevant to a wide range of people."

Source: Jennifer Roccanti, Development Associate, Miriam's Kitchen, Washington, D.C. Phone (202) 452-8926 ext. 223. E-mail: jenn@miriamskitchen.org. Website: www.miriamskitchen.org

Use Fan Pages to Promote Your Cause

Now that fan pages on Facebook (www.facebook.com) are promoting everything from submarine sandwiches to political figures, you may be ready to build one for your organization.

Because Facebook pages can be a hub for other social media programs, they may be even more useful for your supporters than your actual website.

Before creating your Facebook page:

✓ **Spend time navigating other fan pages**. Note how other organizations use Facebook to post announcements and volunteer accomplishments, promote events and share videos. Evaluate comments and suggestions fans make to help determine what you might like to see on your page.

✓ **Make use of discussion forums**. Facebook fan pages have a "wall" where you can post your latest news and announcements. You can allow all users to write on the wall, but directing them to the discussions area may be the best place for your supporters to connect and provide feedback to you and to each other.

✓ **Promote your Facebook page other places**. Once your page is built, create e-mail signatures inviting recipients to "Follow us on Facebook" with a link. Include this in brochures, newsletters and print advertising.

✓ **Determine the purpose for each tab of the page**. Fan pages currently have tabs including the wall, information about your organization, a photo album, the discussion forum and reviews. Decide how you want to use each tab. Have photos, discussions and complete information before promoting your page to the public. When people visit, you want to have useful content for them to browse.

✓ **Remember that fans are different from friends**. You may already have a personal Facebook page where you can share your personal and social life. This is the best place for keeping up with those you allow to be your friends. Fans simply have to become a fan, or like your page. No screening is necessary for fan status. Your organization's icon will appear in a box on every fan's like listing and be seen and possibly accessed by their friends.

Social Networking Concepts

- **Push marketing** — pushing a message out to your constituents that seeks a response (e.g., e-mail messages, text messages, surveys).

- **Pull marketing** — making information available that entices people to pull it from you as needed (e.g., blogging, a mobile Web application).

Giving Up Control Vital to Viral Campaigns

In today's tech-savvy world, word travels fast. When your supporters start texting and tweeting about your special event or fundraiser, and then their friends forward that news to their friends, the campaign has gone viral.

"Giving in to serendipity is part of the entire concept of going viral," says Nonprofit Consultant Ken Goldstein of Goldstein Consulting (Los Gatos, CA). "If a campaign is driven from top-down, with a command and control attitude that was approved in endless closed-door meetings, then by definition it's not viral, no matter how popular or successful it may be."

To be truly viral, Goldstein says, a campaign must be person-to-person sharing out of true interest, "not carefully orchestrated, scheduled and monitored organization-to-masses distribution." Unfortunately, he says this troubles many professional fundraisers and their boards of directors because the very things that make something viral also prevent it from being put in a budget with any accuracy.

The concept of going viral is not new. As long as there have been nonprofits, there have been people-driven efforts to support them, from bake sales to asking for donations in lieu of birthday gifts. "The difference in the social media age is scale," he says. "Instead of supporters bringing in a few hundred dollars from the couple of dozen people they are in physical contact with, the message is quickly forwarded electronically to friends of friends of friends, and the results can be huge."

All nonprofits should be prepared for a fundraising effort, publicity campaign or other communications element to go viral, Goldstein says. To do so, he advises:

- Truly engage friends and followers with social media.

"That means being on Facebook and Twitter with regularly posted updates, including photos of your events and good deeds. You don't just post and run. You listen to what they're saying, and you reply swiftly. Social media is not a broadcast medium; it's a conversation platform."

- Have a large, easy-to-find "Donate Now" button on every page of your website.

- Make your website accessible and easy to read (and donate) from mobile devices. "This includes phones, iPads and whatever is invented next week," says Goldstein.

- Think phones. If your message goes viral, bringing people to your website, and it's not maximized to be read on a phone, and doesn't have a call to action front and center, he says, "You've just blown your opportunity."

Source: Ken Goldstein, Goldstein Consulting. E-mail: ken@goldstein.net

---

Two Viral Campaign Nevers

You may think you know what to do to be prepared for a viral campaign, but do you know what not to do? Nonprofit Consultant Ken Goldstein, Goldstein Consulting (Los Gatos, CA) cites two key elements to keep in mind to make your viral campaign a success:

1. **Never force it.** "Your online audience is message-savvy and knows the difference between a true viral message and being marketed to."

2. **Never correct your supporters.** "If you have somebody sending donors your way, don't yell at them for using the old tag line, or messing with the schedule for your other events or not sending it out to the right people. Only if the message is so off-base or incorrect that you'll end up in legal trouble should you ever get in their way."

Social Media Offers New Twist on Old Campaign

Local health insurance company CDPHP has been a supporter of the Regional Food Bank of Northeastern New York (Latham, NY) for a long time. In fact, they have been doing their CDPHP Holiday Appeal to benefit the food bank for the past nine years, in which they donated $5,000, and then pledged to match donations of $100 or more from other companies up to an additional $5,000.

This year, in honor of the 10th anniversary of the appeal, and in recognition of the increasing importance of social media in promotions and fundraising, the partners decided to add a new twist. CDPHP still offered to match donations of $100 or more up to $5,000, and also offered to donate $5 for every new "like" on the Regional Food Bank's Facebook account up to an additional $5,000. The switch seems to have had an impact. Over $5,000 was raised in addition to

the $10,000 donation from CDPHP. Food Bank Executive Director Mark Quandt says their number of Facebook friends is grew fairly quickly too, largely due to the CDPHP Appeal.

The campaign was widely promoted through local media coverage, area newspaper ads, billboard exposure, mail solicitations of CDPHP's vendors and prior food bank donors and an e-newsletter sent to 2,500 food bank supporters.

All of the funds raised were used for the food bank's BackPack Program, which provides nutritious and easy-to-prepare food to disadvantaged children at times when other resources are not available.

Source: Mark Quandt, Executive Director, Regional Food Bank of Northeastern New York, Latham, NY. Phone (518) 786-3691. E-mail: markq@regionalfoodbank.net.

Press Releases, Social Media Mutually Reinforcing

How would you like to boost your Facebook fans by 177 percent in one week?

That's what happened with Hoops for Hope L.A., a celebrity basketball fundraiser held in February at Los Angeles' Staples Center. The event was a collaboration between two nonprofits in the greater Los Angeles area: The Arnold C. Yoder Survivors Foundation and Hawks Hoops Sports Foundation.

Facebook fans grew as a result of two online press releases embedded with multimedia components such as a YouTube video and a screen capture of the event's Facebook page, and distributed through PRWeb, a company which offers premium search engine optimization and boasts a distribution list of more than 30,000 journalists and bloggers.

"Many people felt that when social media came into play that news releases would be obsolete," says Cheryl Lawson, event specialist with The Perfect Date (Tulsa, OK), who contributed her work pro bono for the L.A. event. "Instead of writing a release, sending it to reporters and hoping for traffic, PRWeb helped us reach the blogging community and other online sources that impact search engine optimization, which drives traffic to our projects."

The first press release drew 1,000 Facebook page views and earned 150 new Facebook fans within 24 hours. The second drove 1,400 page views in the first 24 hours, received nearly 60 retweets on Twitter and drove the event's Facebook fan count past 500.

"The first release created so much excitement among readers that they were looking forward to additional information," says Lawson, explaining why the second release was produced. She says an added benefit of online press releases is that "they stay on the Internet forever," rather than being tossed into a reporters' trash basket after the event ends.

Source: Cheryl Lawson, Founder, The Perfect Date, Tulsa, OK. Phone (478) 227-2789. E-mail: cheryl@theperfect-date.com. Website: www.theperfect-date.com

Content not available in this edition

Link to Social Media Networks

In today's technologically savvy world, tweeting isn't just for the birds.

Even members of Congress use social media like Twitter.com to stay in touch with constituents in real time, sending brief text messages (called tweeting) that can be viewed on the Internet, cell phones and on other portable communications devices.

Facebook, LinkedIn, Flickr and YouTube are just a few of the free online social media sites where you can create an account or group to communicate with existing volunteers and recruit new ones.

To put these social networking tools to use promoting your special event, increase your organization's online presence and boost awareness of your mission:

❑ **Start a Facebook group about your event.** Once you have recruited or identified supporters who already use Facebook, you can send invitations to meetings, post photo albums, give daily progress reports about completed tasks and advertise jobs that still need to be done.

❑ **Tweet messages to spread news.** Your committee meeting has been canceled, but you can't call everyone in time. Twitter allows you to log on to your account and spread the word to many users at once, who can, in turn, notify others of the change in plans.

❑ **Launch a photo album and blog on Flickr.** Some of your volunteers have traveled to Africa on behalf of your organization. Start an account where they can post photos, write about their activities and share links to news with those at home.

❑ **Study social media options for the best fit.** Chances are that many of your volunteers already have accounts on LinkedIn, Twitter, Facebook, YouTube or Flickr. Most of these sites link to each other, so news you share can have a positive ripple effect. Portal websites, like www.socialmediaanswers.com, give tutorials on how to build and cultivate your own network, and describe the benefits of the most popular and versatile services.

Social Media — Can You Measure Its Worth?

Social media is making unforeseen inroads into communications. But what is that traffic worth, in terms of communications, for a nonprofit?

To determine that, we turned to Menachem Wecker, social media expert with The George Washington University (GW), Washington, D.C., and chair of the 2011 Council for Advancement and Support of Education (CASE) Annual Conference for Media Relations Professionals. Wecker is a writer and editor at *George Washington Today,* GW's official online news source, a co-founder of the Association for Social Media and Higher Education at GW, and an active Twitter, LinkedIn and Facebook user and blogger.

Wecker shares what he believes nonprofits should consider when dipping their toes in the pool of social media.

What is the science of measuring cost verses return on social media?

"I would be concerned about any claim that there is a science of measuring the cost versus return on social media. There is certainly a cost, but the return is not often embedded in analytics. Some organizations trumpet 1,000 fans on Facebook as an achievement worthy of a press release. I think a large number of Twitter followers or Facebook fans or blog comments are not necessarily a function of successful use of the medium. The more important question is how well the organization is using social media to integrate into a larger community. That's often a gradual process.

"That said, there is a general rule of thumb that I advise: It is vital to be authentic in social media. Those who have handles on a variety of social media platforms, including Facebook and Twitter, can notoriously sniff out overly congratulatory and institutional language. Social media can be used to lend personality and individuality to your brand, but it can also, when wielded improperly, bore your constituents to tears."

What are the best resources nonprofits can use to help them evaluate their efforts?

"I think nonprofits can learn the most about how well they are doing in their communications strategy by asking their constituents. There are a variety of online tools to track your success, helping you to contextualize your digital footprint, but none of that is as important as talking to real people. If you are communicating properly, you are going to hear positive feedback from the people on the other end of your communications."

> *"Nonprofits can learn the most about how well they are doing in their communications strategy by asking their constituents. There are a variety of online tools to track your success, helping you to contextualize your digital footprint, but none of that is as important as talking to real people."*

What can nonprofits on shoestring budgets do to make the most of their public relations efforts?

"There are a lot of things that don't require a lot of money, if any at all, like staying on top of your institution's Wikipedia page to creating a Twitter handle and a Facebook page. Blogs can be set up for virtually no cost. What is becoming increasingly difficult to buy (even if you have an unlimited budget) are colleagues who have the courage and the curiosity to jump into social networks and explore. If you have people willing to take that plunge, you would be surprised how far a shoestring budget can stretch."

When does it make sense to turn to an outside professional to help with your efforts?

"I think only if you aren't equipped to do it yourself, or if that professional is going to work in concert with your own efforts. New social media tools help curate direct communications. The more links there are in a broken telephone game, the more the message is lost. I'd encourage nonprofits to communicate directly with their constituents. If you only have time to communicate occasionally with your community, then you might consider bringing help in, but not in place of that direct communication."

Source: Menachem Wecker, External Relations, The George Washington University, Washington, D.C. Phone (202) 994-3088. E-mail: mwecker@gwise.gwu.edu. Website: http://www.linkedin.com/in/menachemwecker

Make the Message Match the Audience

Staff at the Performing Arts Workshop (San Francisco, CA) rely on social networking options to communicate important information. Anne Trickey, program and communications coordinator, says she has worked to glean which groups in the organization's constituency respond best to particular types of messaging. She shares some of her findings, and how she uses that information to better match the message to its intended audience:

❑ **Facebook and other social media**: "In our July 2010 newsletter, we sent out a request for our entire database to become fans of (or Like) the Performing Arts Workshop on Facebook (www.facebook.com). We've found it's a good way to get immediate response; people can see pieces of information that give them a good feeling about what we do (and) immediately RSVP to events or comment on what we're doing. It may not be as beautiful to look at as an e-mail newsletter, but an e-mail takes more work to put together — it has to be structured and messaged as a whole. A Facebook post can be brief. Here, we reach a smaller donor base (and) they are most likely to take action on the Internet."

❑ **Traditional mail and word-of-mouth**: "Older donors respond best to this type of communication — which, in our case, is most of our donor base. These donors are more likely to get behind a campaign than the people who are plugged into the Internet, so it's important to speak to them where they will hear it. For them, we focus on results and communicate youth outcomes — success stories from within the community. We involve site partners, schools and communities to communicate how the children are learning '21st century skills, creative expression and self efficacy.' That's our message. It mobilizes people."

❑ **YouTube**: "People who have seen our videos on YouTube (www.youtube.com) tend to be outside of what we think of as our constituency, which is to say we haven't solicited them. But here, we are expanding our pool of supporters, which strengthens the organization." One of the biggest struggles for a group like theirs, she adds, is finding artists who are also great teachers "who understand what we want them to do, and are good in the classroom. When we attract artists who are really engaged in what we do, that gets results. And results attract donors."

Source: Anne Trickey, Program and Communications Coordinator, Performing Arts Workshop, San Francisco, CA. Phone (415) 673-2634. E-mail: anne@performingartsworkshop.org. Website: www.performingartsworkshop.org

---

Seek Donated Video Services

For donated or inexpensive video, troll your community for start-up videography companies and producers seeking to build their portfolios, says Anne Trickey, program and communications coordinator for the Performing Arts Workshop (San Francisco, CA). "The people who put us in touch with our videographers were message-minded and familiar with the language that we use. It was easy to communicate that message to the videographers, and the end product — a combined development and communications effort — turned out really well. We got the product for free, and the videographers got a great example of their work."

Basics of Nonprofit Publicity: Winning Strategies for News Releases, Press Conferences and Media Relations. Edited by Scott C. Stevenson.
© 2011 Stevenson, Inc. Published 2011 by Stevenson, Inc.

Basics of Nonprofit Publicity

RAISING AWARENESS AND BOOSTING COMMUNITY SUPPORT

Nonprofit publicity is often based around the launch of a new program, the construction of a new facility, or the approach of a new fundraising event. This event-driven approach is normal and appropriate, but nonprofits also need to pursue a more low-key, ongoing kind of publicity — the kind that builds awareness over months and years, not weeks and days. The following articles present a variety of approaches related to this kind of publicity.

President's Journal Connects With Members, Community

If building connections within and beyond your membership is a priority, consider a regular newsletter column, monthly e-mail, Web log or other ongoing correspondence written by one or more of your organization's key players.

For four years, Charlotte Keim, president of the Marietta Area Chamber of Commerce (Marietta, OH), has posted her thoughts, insights, dreams for the chamber, plus shared information and feedback from members and movers-and-shakers through her President's Journal, a professional blog hosted on the chamber's website (http://mariettachamber. com/3?newstype=2).

The president's journal features 500- to 600-word essays on topics both occupational and personal. Because the journal is open to the public, its tone differs significantly from other chamber communications, the author notes.

"There is less hard information and more thoughts for reflection and perspective," Keim says. "I try to balance heavy and light, business and nonbusiness, local and regional. To build those personal connections, it helps to have something for everyone."

Recent articles amply demonstrate this variety of subject matter, ranging from the personal "Thankful for Living in Marietta — My Hometown" to the topical "Marietta Chamber Supports Issue 2 & Marietta School Bond" and the historical "Growing Our Economy — A Tale of Marietta From 1921."

For leaders interested in trying such an approach, Keim offers the following tips.

❑ **Don't start if you don't like writing (at least a little)**. "If it's a chore for you to write something, it will be a chore for others to read it," she says.

❑ **Don't commit to a strict schedule**. Though Keim aims for biweekly postings, she recommends a looser approach for those just beginning.

❑ **Write several entries before posting the first**. "Having a bank of five or six articles will give you some breathing room when things get busy."

❑ **Take notes**. "Most people underestimate how difficult it is to think of ideas when staring at a blank piece of paper," Keim says. "Jotting down interesting stories, statistics and bits of news provides a good source of inspiration."

And a final piece of advice? Keep things positive, advises the chamber president. "Everyone has challenges, and that should be acknowledged," Keim says. "But people are looking for hope and optimism, too. That's what they really respond to."

Source: Charlotte Keim, Marietta Area Chamber of Commerce, Marietta, OH. Phone (740) 373-5176. E-mail: keim@ mariettachamber.com. Website: www.mariettachamber.com

Don't Miss A Positive Publicity Opportunity

Don't miss an opportunity to place volunteer-related news. Doing so brings your cause needed visibility and is also a valuable way to recognize your corps of volunteers.

Need some examples of volunteer-related news releases? Try these:

- New volunteer appointments.
- Election of officers with profiles.
- Feature stories of volunteers in action.
- Retiring volunteer profiles.
- Volunteers who have received awards.
- Intergenerational volunteer profiles.
- Volunteering couples' profiles.
- Stories of long-term volunteers celebrating anniversaries of service.

- Youth volunteers.
- Partnerships with businesses and their employees.
- An article including a list of your entire volunteer force to demonstrate your charity's community impact.
- A feature on a collaborative effort between your organization's volunteers and those of another nonprofit.
- Volunteers who make a significant financial contribution to your cause.

New- and Old-school Methods Generate Free Publicity

Press releases and public service announcements are always useful free special-event advertising. Internet social networking sites have opened even more avenues. Combine the two to reach the most people.

❏ **Combine diverse talents on a committee**. Find the best writer, artist and Internet whiz to develop a multi-faceted approach to promoting your event. Brainstorming with experienced volunteers is a productive first step.

❏ **Coordinate online resources for maximum effect**. While Facebook and Twitter are available free to anyone with Internet access, promotional advantages can wither on the vine if nobody is monitoring them. Have one knowledgeable person build an event fan page, place sign-up links in e-mail to volunteers and keep track of RSVPs. Ask another to report results to share with the general committee.

❏ **Use a phone tree and short script**. Ask 50 volunteers to call 10 people with a 30-second narrative to fit most voice mail time limits. "Please join us June 25 at 7 p.m. for the first in a series of three summer concerts at Smith Park Pavilion to benefit The Food Pantry. Tickets are $5 for adults and free for children 12 and under..." Direct them to your website or office for advance purchase and other information.

❏ **Make minifliers to freely distribute**. Create an ad that will fit three to a sheet of letter-sized paper. Ask a printer to donate surplus stock and press time. Contact a direct mail company to see if they will include one in their next mass mailing. Give stacks to volunteers to leave at grocery stores and gas stations and to post on community bulletin boards.

❏ **Encourage community participation**. Offer free admission to those donating good used clothing or toys, a case of canned food or any items that help you reach a goal, like stocking a homeless shelter pantry or funding a children's hospital play room. Most media outlets will help spread the word.

Make the Most of Public Service Announcements

Properly Prepare Your PSA

- Check with each radio or TV station about tape formats, such as 3/4-inch formats for television. Stick to standard time lengths such as 15- and 30-second spots without exceeding the station's limits. The shorter they are, the more frequently they may be used.

- Write or type all copy clearly, and concentrate on name pronunciation. When submitted in a clean, typed format on standard-sized paper (double space to make editing easier), your announcements have a better chance of making it to the air. Use phonetic spelling for hard-to-pronounce names to assist the announcer. Keep length to 75 words or less.

- Submit requests far in advance. TV stations may need three weeks or more, and radio stations appreciate at least two weeks' notice. Notify them immediately of any change in event time or location. You don't want disappointed would-be guests calling the radio station in anger when the announcer didn't have current information.

The saying "Nothing in life is free," may apply to your nonprofit when it comes to public service announcements (PSAs) for radio and television. While radio or TV stations may donate a certain amount of airtime, production costs are usually yours to absorb.

Costs may include models, announcers, sets and film production fees. Are you better off spending money in a more tightly focused advertising vehicle than trying to reach a broad audience? Consider these elements as you plan your PSA:

- **Contemplate the time of day announcement will be broadcast.** Audio and visual media will give the best time slots to clients who pay full retail rates. Public service announcements are usually squeezed in where time permits. If they have a brief shelf life, they may run slightly more frequently. If they are standard announcements, they will be used at random at the discretion of the traffic coordinator or program directors.

- **Consider purchasing airtime at peak times during the day.** If you want to ensure better exposure for your cause and target a portion of your audience demographically, pay for as many spots as budget permits, then ask if the station will run your spots as PSAs during non-peak hours.

- **Learn about the true no-cost options that are available to you.** While commercial air time is precious and costly, most radio and television stations have free community calendars to tell viewers about special area events. Some anchorpersons and radio hosts will read live spots about your events on their programs, eliminating the need to pay production costs for taped versions.

Weigh benefits and shortcomings of PSAs. Ask media outlets for guidelines and preferences and retail rates. With a balanced strategy between paid time and free resources, you may be able to extend your promotion budget to impressive lengths.

Public Service Announcements Instruct, Advertise

Each year, the United Way & Volunteers Services of Greater Yankton (UW & VS), Yankton, SD, and Yankton Volunteer Leaders conduct a clothing drive for those in need. Coordinating efforts with local nonprofits and the help of 50 volunteers, the coat drive has become a smooth operation after 15 years.

Public service announcements (PSAs) play a key role in streamlining the effort, says Pam Kettering, executive director of UW & VS. To steer the efforts of volunteers, her staff produces PSAs for print and radio that instruct the community and volunteers about the clothing drive, including its goals and deadlines. Additionally, a separate PSA informs those in need on how they can obtain the collected hats, mittens and coats.

Kettering advises following these tips for creating clear, concise PSAs that will support your next effort:

- Be clear. Never combine PSAs intended for one audience with information intended for another. Combined PSAs will confuse and distract your audience. One PSA for this clothing drive details steps volunteers and the community need to take to collect donations; a second PSA details how those in need can acquire the items.

- Elicit emotions. Make the community feel the need by appealing to basic needs, desires or emotions to evoke a response from your PSA.

- Create a memorable catch phrase. The goal of the PSA message is to remember the event. An effective PSA sticks in the mind of the audience. Use a powerful phrase or catchy sentence to elicit response.

Source: Pam Kettering, Executive Director, United Way and Volunteer Services of Greater Yankton, Yankton, SD. Phone (605) 665-6766. E-mail: unitedway@iw.net. Website: www.yanktonunitedway.org

Use Anniversaries to Spotlight Historical Milestones

Anniversaries or historical milestones give your organization an entire year in which to remind the community of the contributions you have made through the decades. Some of these ideas may work for your milestone celebrations:

- **Promote your firsts with vintage photos in advertising**. Your first female board chair in 1926 or your first job-training program in 1946 can help tell your story at a glance.

- **Build a time capsule**. Invite the community to watch your representatives fill your time capsule with not only current items, but also treasurers from earlier years that show the evolution of your organization.

- **Craft a community quilt**. Ask area quilters to contribute panels with scenes from events in your history. Hold an unveiling celebration when work is completed.

- **Commission a mural**. Interview local artists to create a visual time line of historical accomplishments. When the

work is finished, make posters and prints to give as gifts or even sell, both framed and unframed.

- **Launch a scholarship program**. Offer college students scholarships that range in size and scope. Name them after people who have been significant in your organization's history, and create a biography or story to go with each award.

- **Introduce a new logo**. Anniversary logos to use with your existing logo boost awareness of your organization's longevity. Use them on apparel, promotional gifts, billboards, advertising and even specialty foods like cupcakes at your open house.

- **Interview past and present supporters**. Look for people whom your organization has helped, such as children, long-term retired employees or volunteers and current staff and supporters to tell what their affiliation with you has meant to them, and how it changed lives for a memorable anniversary video.

Identify and Shout Out Your Organization's Achievements

How much effort do you devote to identifying and spotlighting your organization's most significant achievements?

Constituents (e.g., would-be customers, donors, volunteers) are energized by organizations that can point to significant accomplishments. Yet we sometimes get so wrapped up in carrying out programs and fulfilling our mission that we fail to fully identify and publicize all that we are accomplishing. In fact, we sometimes even fail to realize some of our achievements.

Go through the following steps at least twice each year — or even quarterly — to identify and share your organization's achievements:

1. **Survey each of your organization's departments to determine all their accomplishments.** You may decide to use a form such as the example shown here, visit directly with representatives from each department or both. Whatever method you use, it's important to get department representatives to really share what they have been up to, especially since they may not recognize the significance or newsworthiness of some of their accomplishments.

2. **Assign one employee the responsibility of identifying and researching your organization's most significant achievements.** Researching includes comparing data to other organizations and benchmarking. For example, it's one thing to state, "We served 450 underprivileged youth during the past quarter." It's far more significant to say, "We served 70 percent of our city's underprivileged youth last month. That's a higher percentage than any other city our size throughout the nation."

3. **Follow a plan for getting your accomplishments out to the public.** Categorize your achievements and share them with your CEO and others who meet with the public so they can draw on particular achievements depending on the circumstances. Pitch feature stories to various media outlets regarding particular achievements. Tie your stories to local and national issues that will give the media even more reason to feature your organization.

Remember, it pays to toot your own horn now and then, if you want the public to buy into your organization and its future accomplishments.

ACCOMPLISHMENTS SURVEY

This quarterly survey is intended to bring any and all achievements to everyone's awareness. As you complete the survey, think about your department's work during the past three months. How has employee time been focused? What has been accomplished during that time? Remember, there are no wrong answers.

The information you provide may or may not be shared with the public. The form in which it is shared will be determined by the Office of Media Relations.

Please take a few minutes to complete this survey and return it to the Office of Media Relations within the next few days. Thanks for your valuable assistance.

Your Name _____   Department _____
Phone _____   Date_____

Key areas our department has been focusing during the past three months:
1. _____
2. _____
3. _____
4. _____
5. _____

In my opinion, my department's biggest recent accomplishments include:
1. _____   4. _____
2. _____   5. _____
3. _____   6. _____

When I think of [Name of Organization], I'm most proud of:

Based on our department's work and responsibilities, here's something that others (employees and/or the public) may not realize:

Can you think of any local, regional or national issues that relate directly or indirectly to accomplishments within your department? Please share them:

❑ Local issue   ❑ Regional issue   ❑ National issue

Here's how our work and accomplishments are related to this issue:

Assemble a Public Relations Advisory Committee

A volunteer public relations advisory committee can be worth its weight in gold in terms of community and media relations. Be creative and open-minded to find individuals who can attract the spotlight to your organization in a positive way.

To help you create a committee that includes a balanced group of professionals who will bring positive visibility to your cause, seek out candidates who possess communication skills, media savviness and the ability to persuade and inspire others. To do so:

- **Explore creative or marketing staff of large organizations who already support you.** A major business or institution with in-house marketing and public relations may have skilled volunteers to loan to you — graphic designers, copywriters, media coordinators or photographers.

- **Seek out small business owners.** These men and women must often oversee marketing efforts for their own businesses, including advertising development, community relations and promotion. They are likely to know account executives from a variety of media sources, which may be useful to you as well.

- **Keep a watch for the newly retired.** News anchors, television and newspaper reporters and advertising agency execs in your community may be ready to retire and do volunteer work on your behalf.

- **Think of the most effective sales persons you know.** A real estate agent, insurance planner or corporate sales director will be comfortable making calls, persuading media to attend your next event and preparing presentations or proposals.

Opportunities Abound for Public Relations Committee

Your organization's board has a well-rounded, respected public relations committee of volunteers. Each member is ready to use his/her skills and contacts to help enhance your charity's image and educate the community about your services.

Now what do you do with all of this talent? How can you respect these individuals' time while still reaping maximum, continuous benefit?

Here are some worthwhile ways to put your PR committee to work:

- **Ask them to speak to various groups about your organization.** Provide them with brochures, videos and contact information — including links to your social media connections — when they are guest speakers in the community.

- **Invite them to scout for sponsors for your events.** Committee members may be aware of other business execs who, for their own public relations reasons, want to sponsor a worthy project or event. Ask if they would be willing to contact three potential sponsors or in-kind donors each month.

- **Encourage regular creativity with group meetings.** If your public relations committee meets at least quarterly, ask each member to arrive with a promotion idea for one of your programs.

- **Request yearly image assessments.** These committee members will hear feedback about your organization that you, as paid staff, may not hear. Ask for an oral or written assessment from each, pointing out image strengths and weaknesses.

- **Invite committee members to write letters to other**

community leaders and businesses. Make the letters friendly and informative without asking for money at this time. Your members can write it in their own words, telling the reader why they value involvement in your organization, and invite them to do the same.

- **Assign thank-you calls to your committee.** Your supporters will enjoy getting regular calls from friendly ambassadors who simply want to express appreciation for past contributions, not ask for more donations at this time.

- **Charge members to serve as ambassadors at large.** Word-of-mouth is one of the most effective ways to spread good news about your organization. Request that each member tell one or two friends a week about one of your programs or services.

- **Invite them to look for promotional opportunities in their neighborhoods.** Each member of the committee is loyal to certain retailers — grocery stores, gas stations and dry cleaners. Would those stores that your committee members patronize make brochures available or post some announcements for your cause?

- **Give committee members responsibility for developing promotion ideas** and volunteering for the job(s) they would enjoy doing themselves, or suggesting the name of a new volunteer to assist.

- **Assign committee members to serve as your media spokespersons at appropriate times.** When it's time for a radio or TV interview about your institution or special event, ask one or two of your most skilled committee members to be spokespersons. Enthusiastic words from a volunteer may be more meaningful to the audience.

Share Your Strategic Plan With the Public

Your nonprofit recently developed a five-year strategic plan that includes exciting new programs and facility expansion. Those who participated in shaping the plan — staff, board members, key donors and volunteers — share your enthusiasm for what can be realized if everything falls into place.

But what about the public at large? How can you make them aware of your strategic plan in a way that will excite and engage them? Here are a handful of ideas for doing so:

1. Host a series of small group, information-sharing meetings in which you summarize plans for your organization's future and offer facility tours, explaining changes that will come about as your plan is realized.

2. Get key members of the strategic planning committee to submit editorials that share a glimpse into what the future will hold for your organization and those you serve.

3. Share your strategic plan, or portions of it, on your website.

4. Incorporate comments about your strategic plans into all public speeches.

5. Pitch an occasional feature idea to the media about some aspect of your organization's future: why you have chosen to address a particular issue, how you intend to go about doing it and the impact it will have on the community and those you serve.

> **Announce Your Plan's Progress**
>
> Use tools and metrics to monitor the progress of your strategic plan. Then share that progress with the public on an annual basis.

How to Get Free PR Expertise

Like many communications directors at nonprofit organizations, you are expected to wear a number of hats in areas that are sometimes outside the realm of your formal expertise.

Your department may not have a budget for hiring outside public relations consultants, but making proper contacts through community networking events may help you develop a go-to list of experts who can advise you for little or no cost.

- **Join your local chamber of commerce.** Most of them hold mixing events and membership luncheons where you can meet public relations professionals. Some also offer free or low-cost seminars where owners of public relations firms offer advice.

- **Become involved in organizations complementing your own.** As a volunteer for institutions who do have public relations departments, you may find colleagues who are willing to share ideas.

- **Develop a partnership.** Team up with a public relations firm that seeks an alliance with a nonprofit cause specifically so they can add volunteer activities to their own company resumes. Most public relations firms choose one or two local causes to support with gratis services — convince them that yours should be one of them.

- **Look online for PR firm websites.** Even if you have to wade through websites promising something for nothing to get to the meat, there are plentiful resources with public relations strategies, advice and free subscriptions to e-newsletters.

- **Subscribe to professional journals.** Just because you're not an official public relations professional doesn't mean that you can't buy magazines, journals or newsletters written for them.

- **Ask a PR professional to join your board.** Do some research to see which public relations professionals in your area are most likely to be supportive of your organization's mission. Invite them to have lunch, take a tour of your facility and see your programs in action. Ask them how your organization might help increase community awareness of your services and show them specific ways their involvement on your board will be mutually beneficial.